Discipline With Heart

A Parent's Guide to Nurturing Will, Wisdom, and Joy in Family Life

Grace Whitaker

© Copyright 2024 - All rights reserved.

The content contained within this book may not be reproduced, duplicated or transmitted without direct written permission from the author or the publisher.

Under no circumstances will any blame or legal responsibility be held against the publisher, or author, for any damages, reparation, or monetary loss due to the information contained within this book, either directly or indirectly.

Legal Notice:

This book is copyright protected. It is only for personal use. You cannot amend, distribute, sell, use, quote or paraphrase any part, or the content within this book, without the consent of the author or publisher.

Disclaimer Notice:

Please note the information contained within this document is for educational and entertainment purposes only. All effort has been executed to present accurate, up to date, reliable, complete information. No warranties of any kind are declared or implied. Readers acknowledge that the author is not engaged in the rendering of legal, financial, medical or professional advice. The content within this book has been derived from various sources. Please consult a licensed professional before attempting any techniques outlined in this book.

By reading this document, the reader agrees that under no circumstances is the author responsible for any losses, direct or indirect, that are incurred as a result of the use of the information contained within this document, including, but not limited to, errors, omissions, or inaccuracies.

Table of Contents

INTRODUCTION 1
    THE ESSENCE OF PARENTING 2
    THE SCIENCE BEHIND CHILDREN'S BEHAVIORS 2

PART I: FOUNDATIONS OF HEART-CENTERED DISCIPLINE 5
    CHAPTER 1: UNDERSTANDING YOUR CHILD 7
        The Developing Mind: What Science Tells Us 8
        Emotional Landscapes: Navigating Moods and Reactions 11
        Setting Realistic Expectations: Age-Appropriate Behaviors and Milestones 13
        Cultivating an Environment of Connection and Love 17
    CHAPTER 2: THE PHILOSOPHY OF "DISCIPLINE WITH HEART" 19
        Beyond Punishment: The Meaning of Discipline 19
        The Essence of Heart-Centered Discipline 20
        The Power of Connection: Building Trust and Understanding ... 22
        Principles of Heart-Centered Discipline 25
        Implementing Heart-Centered Discipline Principles 26
        Embracing the Discipline With Heart Principles 28

PART II: THE DISCIPLINE SPECTRUM 29
    CHAPTER 3: GENTLE GUIDANCE—EXPLORING SOFT-TOUCH STRATEGIES 31
        The Role of Empathy and Understanding 31
        Nonverbal Communication: The Art of Gentle Guidance 35
        Positive Reinforcement Techniques 37
        Gentle Guidance in Action 39
    CHAPTER 4: FIRM BOUNDARIES—ESTABLISHING LIMITS WITH LOVE 41
        The Importance of Consistency and Clarity 41
        Reinforcing Boundaries 44
        Setting Clear House Rules 46
        Balancing Freedom With Responsibility 48
        Nurturing Independence While Maintaining Boundaries 49
    CHAPTER 5: CREATIVE SOLUTIONS—THINKING OUTSIDE THE BOX 51
        Engaging Cooperation and Creativity 51
        Developing Problem-Solving Skills 54
        Incorporating Play Into Discipline 57
        Thinking Outside the Box 61

PART III: KEY THEMES IN HEART-CENTERED DISCIPLINE 63

Chapter 6: Forgiveness and Healing 65
- The Role of Forgiveness in Parenting 66
- Teaching Kids About Forgiveness 69
- Steps to Genuine Apologies 71
- Healing From Family Conflict 73
- Modeling Forgiveness 75

Chapter 7: Celebrating the Positive 77
- Shifting Focus: Recognizing and Reinforcing Positive Behaviors 78
- Creating a Culture of Gratitude at Home 81
- Daily Rituals That Promote Joy 82
- Recognizing Good Behavior 85

Chapter 8: Seeking and Offering Support 87
- When to Seek Professional Help 88
- Building a Support Network: Community Resources and Peer Support 90
- Developing Open Lines of Communication 92
- Building Essential Skills Through Networking 95

PART IV: IMPLEMENTING DISCIPLINE WITH HEART 97

Chapter 9: Practical Wisdom—Bringing It All Together 99
- Applying Practical Wisdom 99
- Day-to-Day Scenarios and Solutions 101
- Customizing the Approach to Fit Your Family 104
- Troubleshooting Common Challenges 105
- Implementing Heart-Centered Discipline Strategies 108

Chapter 10: Growing Together—Evolving as a Family 111
- Navigating Changes and Challenges 112
- Continuing the Journey of Heart-Centered Discipline 114
- Implementing Heartfelt Discipline Principles Effectively 116
- Adapting to Each Developmental Stage 117
- Embracing Change 120

CONCLUSION 121

REFERENCES 125

Introduction

I wholeheartedly believe that when we are fully engaged in parenting, regardless of how imperfect, vulnerable, and messy it is, we are creating something sacred. –
Brené Brown

I remember one evening when I was growing up, I had just broken a vase while running indoors—a rule I knew I was not supposed to break. Instead of yelling or sending me to my room, my mother sat me down at the kitchen table and asked me calmly, "Why do you think we ask you not to run in the house?" I mumbled something about them not wanting things to get broken, but her gentle prodding led me to realize it wasn't just about the vase—it was about respect for the home and others' spaces.

That simple conversation became a turning point in how I understood discipline. It wasn't about punishment; it was about learning. Discipline, when done with heart, doesn't stifle a child's will but instead guides them toward wisdom. It teaches them to understand consequences, develop empathy, and grow into adults who are not simply obedient but thoughtful and joyful in their choices.

Parenting comes with a range of challenges, joys, and uncertainties, as well as moments of deep insight. The choices we make during the early years of our child's development are crucial in shaping their future and influencing their character and ability to navigate the world. As a parent, it's natural to experience guilt and self-doubt, questioning whether you're doing enough or doing it right. Balancing discipline with maintaining a deep connection with your children can feel like walking a tightrope. There's often a fear of creating trauma or doing something that might leave a lasting negative impact. And of course, feeling overwhelmed or burned out is all too common, especially when there's so much at stake. I've faced these challenges firsthand, and I understand the emotional toll they take.

Child development can be difficult to comprehend, but having a helpful ally can make a big difference. This book is a valuable resource for gaining practical insights and strategies rooted in kindness, empathy, and respect. By using these approaches, navigating the complexities of child development will become more manageable and rewarding.

The Essence of Parenting

At its core, parenting is an evolving art, one that demands both intuition and knowledge. Whether you're a new parent, full of excitement and anxiety about caring for a newborn, or an experienced parent seeking to refine your approach, understanding the science behind your child's development can be immensely empowering.

Knowing how the developing mind works is crucial for effective parenting. Kids' brains are constantly growing and changing, which directly affects their behaviors and emotions. By gaining insight into the science of brain development, you can understand why your kids exhibit certain behaviors at different stages. Understanding the critical milestones in brain growth will help you anticipate what to expect and when—enabling you to respond in a more tailored and effective manner.

The Science Behind Children's Behaviors

If you've ever wondered why your child acts a certain way, neurologically, children's emotions and behaviors are heavily influenced by neurotransmitters like serotonin and dopamine (Kim et al., 2023). These chemicals are responsible for regulating mood and behavior, so understanding how neurotransmitters work will equip you to support your children's emotional well-being. Once you recognize that many reactions result from chemical responses rather than willful defiance, you will be able to be patient and adapt your expectations accordingly.

This scientific perspective on behavior can help you develop discipline strategies that are compassionate and effective.

The environment kids grow up in also plays a key role in shaping their brain development. Creating a supportive and stimulating environment promotes cognitive development and encourages good behavior. For example, sharing your feelings with your kids honestly and appropriately allows them to do the same, and also cultivates a more positive environment. By expressing your emotions healthily, you model to your kids how they can effectively articulate their feelings, and also validate the importance of acknowledging those feelings. On the other hand, recognizing the negative effects of a less nurturing environment can prompt you to come up with proactive measures to promote healthier growth.

Understanding your children's emotions is key to effective parenting. Emotions play a huge role in how children act, and identifying and responding to your child's various emotional states is important. Whether they feel frustrated, angry, or sad, recognizing and addressing these feelings can help validate their emotions. As children grow, they naturally develop better emotional regulation skills. However, this development doesn't happen at the same pace for everyone. By appreciating and accepting these individual differences, you can better support your children in navigating their emotions. Providing age-appropriate strategies for managing their emotions can empower your kids to handle their feelings positively and constructively.

Children also develop at their own pace in all aspects of life, and recognizing this is crucial. Taking a patient approach during times of slow progress can deepen your bond. By understanding typical behaviors for your child's age, you can turn moments of frustration into opportunities for support, keeping a positive connection even in difficult times. Remember, every child has unique qualities that shape how they engage with the world around them: Some kids are more sensitive by nature, while others tend to be more extroverted. Recognizing and embracing these differences to better cater to your child's specific needs is key, while flexibility and adaptability can help you create effective discipline strategies.

Parenting is an inspiring journey of personal growth; it's about learning not only how to guide and nurture your kids but also how to evolve alongside them. As you teach your children, you will discover more about your own strengths, limitations, and values. This process encourages patience, resilience, and emotional intelligence, with the challenges you face prompting self-reflection and adaptation.

As you incorporate the insights shared in this book, you will cultivate a nurturing environment that prioritizes emotional well-being, encourages collaboration, and creates a harmonious home environment.

Part I:
Foundations of Heart-Centered Discipline

Chapter 1:
Understanding Your Child

We worry about what a child will become tomorrow, yet we forget that he is someone today. –Stacia Tauscher

It was a sunny Saturday morning, and I was feeling pretty confident about my parenting skills. I'd just read an article about letting toddlers explore their independence and engage in sensory experiences. So, I set my son Max up in his high chair, gave him a bowl of fresh blueberries, and thought, *This will be a nice, calm activity.*

Well, what I hadn't considered was Max's commitment to experimentation and chaos. Within minutes, those blueberries had become his new artistic medium. There were squashed blueberries on his cheeks, blueberries in his hair, and blueberries splattered across the floor. At one point, I swear he tried to see if he could throw one with the same trajectory as a major league pitcher. The grand finale? He smashed a handful against the wall and giggled like he'd just solved a physics equation.

I stood there, stunned, covered in blueberry juice, and thinking, *Why didn't anyone tell me toddlers are secret anarchists?* But in that moment, I realized this was a part of his development. His brain was wired for discovery and cause-and-effect learning, and my kitchen was just the unfortunate laboratory.

A child's development can be messy, unpredictable, and sometimes downright confusing. But understanding what's happening behind those seemingly chaotic moments is key to nurturing your kid through each stage. Whether it's blueberry explosions or temper tantrums, there's something deeper happening.

Understanding your child involves exploring the fascinating world of their development, which can provide valuable insights. When you recognize the different stages of neurological and psychological growth, you can adapt your parenting techniques and effectively discipline and support your kids.

The Developing Mind: What Science Tells Us

If you've ever wondered why your child acts in a particular manner, the answer lies in neuroplasticity—the brain's ability to adapt and develop over time. Understanding children's neurological and psychological development is crucial for creating successful discipline strategies. By learning how a child's brain matures, you can adjust your methods to meet their developmental needs.

Brain Development Milestones

During the first few years of a child's life, their brain experiences rapid growth and change. Throughout infancy and early childhood, the brain constantly forms new neural connections at an incredible pace (Center on the Developing Child, n.d.). During this period, the brain goes through synaptic pruning and myelination, which help enhance brain functions and increase efficiency. These processes are crucial in shaping a child's cognitive abilities and setting the stage for future learning and development, ensuring the brain operates more efficiently and effectively by strengthening neural connections and enhancing cognitive function.

Understanding these stages can help you appreciate that younger kids may struggle with impulse control because their prefrontal cortex—the area responsible for decision-making and self-regulation—is still developing. Recognizing this helps you adjust your expectations and responses, choosing guidance and support over punishment.

In addition, being aware of the flexibility of a child's developing brain can help you address behavioral issues. For example, instead of scolding your child for not sharing, you can concentrate on teaching them how to play cooperatively with others. Actively guiding children through these learning experiences helps improve their behavior and builds a stronger parent–child relationship.

Also, acknowledging the different stages of child development can help you navigate challenging situations with empathy and patience. For example, you will start viewing toddler tantrums as a natural part of their growth and development. By staying calm and focusing on the root emotional need behind the tantrum, you can respond with understanding and support rather than reacting with frustration or punishment.

The Role of Neurotransmitters

Neurotransmitters (chemicals that help transmit signals between neurons in the brain), such as dopamine and serotonin, help regulate emotions and behaviors. Dopamine is associated with pleasure and reward, influencing motivation and attention; meanwhile, serotonin impacts mood regulation and social behavior. Understanding the role of these chemicals can help you develop effective discipline strategies. For example, rewarding positive behavior can increase dopamine levels, which promotes a sense of accomplishment and encourages kids to repeat the desired behavior. On the other hand, appreciating how low serotonin levels contribute to irritability will encourage you to use calming techniques to defuse conflict rather than intensify it.

As a parent, understanding how neurotransmitters impact your kids' well-being can help you maintain a balanced lifestyle. Ensuring your children get enough sleep, eat nutritious food, and stay active is crucial for keeping these chemicals in check and supporting good mental health.

Impact of Environment on Brain Development

The environment children grow up in can significantly impact their brain development. A nurturing setting with sensory stimulation, social interaction, and learning opportunities encourages healthy growth. In contrast, a stressful environment characterized by neglect or abuse can hinder development and contribute to long-term behavioral and emotional challenges.

Creating an enriching environment for your children by involving them in activities that stimulate their cognitive and emotional growth is essential. Simple activities like reading, playing, and exploring nature offer the kind of stimulation that supports healthy brain development. Equally important is fostering a loving and supportive atmosphere where children feel safe and secure, helping them build resilience and adaptability.

Cultivating a nurturing environment also involves minimizing stress, which can negatively impact a child's brain development and growth. You can reduce stress by creating regular schedules, providing reliable care, and showing your kids how to handle stress positively.

The Science of Play

Think back to the games you enjoyed as a child—those simple yet captivating activities that brought you hours of fun and joy. Play is essential for cognitive and emotional development. It stimulates different parts of the brain, leading to better connections between neurons and improved brain function. Allowing children to choose their activities enhances their creativity and critical thinking skills. Additionally, engaging in active play that includes physical movement can help them develop their motor skills and coordination.

Studies show that play can increase the production of dopamine and gamma-aminobutyric acid (GABA). These chemicals are responsible for the wiring of the prefrontal cortex and enhancing executive control systems. In other words, incorporating regular playtime into a child's routine can positively impact their emotional regulation, problem-solving skills, and information-processing speed (Elbeltagi et al., 2023).

Additionally, engaging in play activities encourages the development of whole-brain integration, improving sensory processing. For example, activities like building blocks, pretend play, and outdoor games stimulate the logical, analytical left hemisphere and the creative, expressive right hemisphere of the brain (Williamson, 2023). This balance of cognitive functions improves cognitive abilities and overall brain health.

Emotional Landscapes: Navigating Moods and Reactions

Recognizing a child's emotional cues is the first step toward understanding their thoughts and feelings. Children often express their feelings through facial expressions, body language, and actions long before they can articulate them in words. For example, when a child clenches their fists and furrows their brow, they might be experiencing frustration or anger. You can observe these subtle signs to gauge your child's feelings. Approach these observations with empathy and curiosity rather than judgment. Asking open-ended questions like "I see you're clenching your fists. Are you feeling upset?" can help children identify and label their emotions. This empathetic approach validates their feelings and encourages them to open up about their experiences.

As children grow, their ability to regulate their emotions changes as well. Younger children tend to grapple more with emotional regulation because their brains are still developing the necessary skills. Tantrums and meltdowns are frequent, and are often signs that a child feels overwhelmed and has difficulty managing their emotions. Over time, with guidance and positive role modeling, kids can learn to understand and regulate their emotions more effectively.

Children learn about emotional regulation from their parents. When you handle stress calmly, your kids are likely to follow your example. For instance, if you feel overwhelmed, saying, "I'm feeling a bit stressed right now, so I'm going to take some deep breaths" allows your children to see firsthand how emotions can be managed effectively. Simple techniques such as deep breathing, counting to 10, or engaging in a favorite calming activity can help you learn how to handle stress.

Let's look at a few strategies to help kids develop emotional regulation skills.

Conduct Regular Emotional Check-Ins

Regular emotional check-ins can create a safe space for children to share their feelings. Setting aside dedicated time each day or week for these check-ins can help make talking about emotions a regular part of family life. This practice can be as simple as talking on your way home from school or as structured as holding a weekly family meeting. Starting the conversation with prompts like "What was the best part of your day?" or "Is there anything that made you feel sad today?" can encourage your children to reflect on their experiences and express their feelings openly.

Talk About Emotions Openly

Having open conversations about emotions can help kids understand and regulate them. You can take advantage of instances where your children experience emotional difficulties to help them learn about self-awareness and how to manage their feelings. For instance, when your child has a meltdown, instead of rushing to calm them down, you can use it as a teachable moment. You could say, "I see you're upset right now. Let's take a minute to calm down together, and then we can talk about what's bothering you."

Understand Sensory Needs

Understanding your own sensory needs is as important as understanding those of your kids. We all have unique sensory preferences that influence how we respond to stress and emotions. Recognizing these differences can help you tailor your approaches to support your child's emotional needs. For instance, some children may find comfort in physical touch, like hugs, during moments of distress, while others might need a quiet space to calm down. Working together and learning to tune into your kids' sensory needs will allow you to support their emotional well-being.

Recognize Your Emotional Triggers

Recognizing emotional triggers and biases that stem from your upbringing is crucial in parenting. Many of us learned to suppress certain emotions based on societal or familial expectations, and these learned habits influence how we react to our children's emotional outbursts. Reflecting on your emotional history and working through any biases can help you respond empathetically to your children's needs.

Parenting is a full-time job that requires you to practice self-care regularly to maintain your emotional well-being. Taking time to recharge will enhance your efficiency. Self-care looks different for everyone; it might involve physical activities like exercise, or more relaxing practices like meditation or reading. Prioritizing your well-being is a great way to teach your kids the importance of self-care, showing them that it's okay to take time for yourself.

Setting Realistic Expectations: Age-Appropriate Behaviors and Milestones

As parents, we naturally want the best for our children—setting goals, encouraging growth, and helping them reach their full potential. But keep in mind that every child develops at their own pace. Understanding age-appropriate behaviors and developmental milestones is key to setting realistic expectations and encourages an environment of patience and support. When you align your expectations with your child's growth stage, you reduce frustration and nurture their unique abilities.

Understanding Developmental Milestones

While kids develop at their own unique pace, there are general milestones that can give you a sense of what to expect at various stages. These milestones include physical, cognitive, speech–language, and social–emotional development from infancy through adolescence.

At around three months, most babies can lift their heads and start to make babbling sounds. From six months, some start learning to sit on their own, and by their first birthday, they start taking their first steps and saying simple words like "mama" or "dada." As children grow into toddlers, their language skills continue to develop, and they begin forming short sentences (Rodgers, n.d.). They also improve their motor skills, allowing them to run, climb, and play independently.

Preschoolers, aged three to five years, experience significant growth in their social–emotional abilities. During this stage, they start to understand the concept of sharing, show empathy toward others, and follow complex instructions. Additionally, their cognitive abilities improve as they learn to count, recognize letters, and solve basic puzzles.

As children progress through elementary school, they further develop their foundational skills. At this stage, they start to gain a sense of independence, form friendships, and understand right from wrong. Their cognitive abilities also improve and they become better at solving problems and focusing on tasks. They also become more logical when dealing with everyday situations.

During adolescence, kids go through significant changes as puberty sets in. They experience rapid physical growth, emotional turmoil, and heightened cognitive development. Teenagers start to shape their own identities, challenge existing norms and beliefs, and develop a sense of autonomy (Stanford Medical Children's Health, n.d.).

Understanding these stages can help you establish reasonable expectations and support your kids on their growth journey.

The Importance of Patience

Kids have a way of pushing your limits at times—for instance, when they throw a tantrum or refuse to listen. However, patience is a crucial part of parenting. Remember, children don't develop uniformly, and some may reach milestones sooner or later than others. It's important not to compare your kids to their peers; instead, focus on your child's unique journey and celebrate their progress.

Patience allows you to do the following:

- **Create a supportive environment where your kids feel safe to explore and make mistakes:** Positive reinforcement works wonders here. Celebrate small victories and encourage them when they encounter setbacks. This helps build their confidence and resilience, qualities that will serve them well throughout their lifetime.

- **Understand your kid's emotional needs:** It's normal for kids to test your patience, sometimes causing you to lose your cool. As parents, the way we react to our children is often influenced by our past experiences and how we were raised. When dealing with difficult behavior, patience can help you respond calmly instead of reacting impulsively. Take tantrums, for example, which are common among toddlers. Rather than seeing them as misbehavior, try to understand that tantrums are often a way for children to express frustration or communicate unmet needs. By staying patient in these moments, you can address the root cause of the behavior and teach your kids healthier ways to express their emotions.

Tailoring Expectations to Temperament

Every child has a unique temperament that affects how they interact with the world. Recognizing and understanding your child's temperament can help you tailor your expectations and parenting strategies effectively.

Temperament includes factors like activity level, adaptability, intensity of reactions, and mood. Some children are easygoing and adapt well to changes, while others may be highly sensitive and require more time to adjust. Categorizing your children's temperaments into broad categories—easy or flexible, active or feisty, and slow to warm up or cautious—will give you valuable insights into their behavior and needs.

For example, an easy child who adapts quickly to new situations might do well in a lively environment with plenty of social interactions. On the other hand, a slow-to-warm-up child might need a more gradual introduction to new experiences. Understanding these differences will allow you to create an environment where your kids can thrive and feel at ease.

Reducing friction and increasing cooperation requires aligning your parenting approach with your child's temperament. If you have a high-energy, feisty child, incorporating opportunities for physical activity can be a helpful way to channel their energy in a positive direction. On the other hand, more cautious children may thrive in environments with predictable routines that offer a sense of security and stability.

Flexibility in Your Approach

Being flexible in your parenting approach is crucial, because what works for one child might not work for another—even within the same family. So, as your kids grow, you may need to adapt your disciplinary methods accordingly. While time-outs may work well for younger children, older children may respond better to discussions about consequences and problem-solving strategies. The key is to find an approach that resonates with your child and achieves the desired results.

Flexibility also involves being open to trying new techniques and learning from your experiences. Parenting strategies are constantly evolving, and new research often emerges, making it essential to adjust and adapt as needed. If one strategy isn't working, try a different approach. Showing kids that problem-solving is a constant process teaches them to be resilient and creative when faced with challenges.

Additionally, flexibility can help you handle external factors that may influence your children's well-being. For instance, changes in the family structure, school environment, or social interactions can all affect children's development. Adaptability can help you handle these changes gracefully, providing stability and support for your kids' needs during transition periods.

Cultivating an Environment of Connection and Love

Understanding the complex process of your child's neurological and psychological development is key to implementing thoughtful and effective discipline strategies. Recognizing key factors like brain development milestones, the role of neurotransmitters, and how the environment can shape brain growth will give you deeper insight into your kids' growth and development, allowing you to create compassionate and tailored approaches to discipline.

As you journey through the different developmental stages, remember that each phase brings its own unique challenges, joys, and growth opportunities. Recognizing the milestones, emotional needs, and cognitive changes your kids experience will help you create a foundation of empathy and insight. This knowledge will empower you to meet your kids where they are, cultivating an environment of connection, security, and love. However, understanding is just the beginning. How you guide your children through these stages is equally important.

In the next chapter, we will explore the philosophy of "discipline with heart," a compassionate approach to nurturing your child's will and wisdom while maintaining the joy of family life. This philosophy offers practical tools for balancing structure and support, empowering you to guide your kids in a way that strengthens your relationship and encourages emotional growth.

Chapter 2:
The Philosophy of "Discipline With Heart"

The point of parenting isn't to have all the answers before we start out, but instead to figure it out on the go as our children grow, because as they do, so will we. –
Bridgett Miller

Parenting is often portrayed as a set of rigid rules to follow, but what if we looked at it as a graceful dance instead? Picture it as a delicate balance of forming connections, offering guidance, and showering love on your children. Discipline shouldn't be seen as a means of control but rather as a way to impart valuable lessons, nurture growth, and lay the groundwork for your children's future wisdom.

In a world filled with conflicting advice and societal pressures, it's easy to lose sight of the true essence of discipline. You may struggle to find the right balance between being an authoritative figure and a gentle guide, fearing that you may come on too strong.

Discipline with heart means guiding children through empathy and understanding rather than fear. Traditional approaches often focus on punishment, which can damage relationships and make children more likely to hide their mistakes. Heart-centered discipline shifts the focus to building trust and connection, recognizing that discipline should be a collaborative process that focuses on teaching children rather than controlling them. By making it a priority to meet your children's emotional needs and create a nurturing environment, you can help them grow and thrive.

Beyond Punishment: The Meaning of Discipline

Discipline is often equated with punishment, but true discipline goes beyond merely correcting behavior. At its core, discipline is about teaching and guiding children toward becoming responsible, empathetic, and self-aware individuals.

Heart-centered discipline reframes discipline as an opportunity to teach, not punish. Rather than focusing on what a child has done wrong, it emphasizes understanding why a behavior occurred in the first place. This approach asks: What unmet need or emotion is driving this behavior? How can I, as a parent address that need and help my child grow through it? Discipline, in this light, becomes a way to nurture a child's development—not by instilling fear, but by cultivating self-awareness, empathy, and personal responsibility.

The aim of discipline, then, is not compliance but empowerment. It's about equipping children with the tools to make better decisions. When discipline is rooted in the heart, it teaches children the value of connection, responsibility, and emotional intelligence, which will serve them throughout their lives.

The Essence of Heart-Centered Discipline

Traditional punitive measures, such as time-outs, detentions, or even physical reprimands, often aim to invoke fear as a deterrent to unwanted behavior. However, fear-based tactics can lead kids to focus on avoiding punishment rather than understanding why their actions were wrong.

When you discipline kids out of fear, you miss out on the chance to build trust and create a strong connection with them. Instead of understanding the reasons behind your rules, they may simply obey out of fear and anxiety. This kind of discipline can lead them to hide their mistakes or lie to avoid getting in trouble rather than feeling comfortable being honest and open with you. Over time, this can diminish trust, making it difficult to effectively address future disciplinary issues.

Changing your perspective on misbehavior is another key aspect of heart-centered discipline. When a child acts out, it's not always because they're being purposely bad. Misbehavior could be a sign of unmet needs, emotional dysregulation, or developmental challenges, and could therefore be an opportunity for them to learn and grow. For example, if a child acts out because they feel overwhelmed by schoolwork, addressing the root cause—perhaps by providing additional support or easing their workload—can help them behave better in the long run. This both addresses the current problem and teaches kids how to handle similar challenges in the future, helping them build resilience and develop emotional intelligence.

To effectively implement heart-centered discipline, set up a solid framework. This means creating routines and laying out what's expected of your kids, which will make them feel more secure and less likely to act out. Children thrive in environments that are predictable and structured because it gives them a sense of safety and belonging. When routines are disrupted or expectations are unclear, they often become anxious or confused, leading to increased behavioral issues.

Creating a Discipline Plan

A good discipline plan involves setting age-appropriate boundaries and sticking to them, while also being kind and understanding. It's crucial to talk to your child about these rules so they know why they're in place. For example, explaining why going to bed at a certain time is important for staying healthy and getting enough rest can help your child see why it's necessary to follow that rule.

The Role of Positive Reinforcement In Discipline

Within this framework, positive reinforcement plays a vital role. Acknowledging and celebrating your children's efforts and achievements reinforces desired behaviors and encourages them to keep doing their best and aiming for positive outcomes. When giving praise, ensure it's specific and meaningful, focusing on the value of the behavior itself rather than just giving a general compliment. For instance, instead of saying, "Good job," you could say something like, "I saw how well you waited for your turn today; you showed a lot of self-control." Giving kids specific feedback on their behavior helps them build confidence and reinforces good behavior.

Implementing Logical Consequences

When kids misbehave, it's important to implement logical consequences to help them learn from their actions. Logical consequences are directly connected to the misbehavior and show children the repercussions of their choices. For instance, if a child purposefully spills their milk, a logical consequence would be having them clean up the mess. This teaches them to take responsibility for their actions and shows them the impact of their actions.

Restorative Practices

Implementing restorative practices can make discipline more effective. Restorative practices mend relationships rather than just punishing someone. Mediated dialogues and conflict-resolution sessions allow kids to talk about their feelings, see things from another point of view, and work together to solve problems. These techniques don't just solve the current issue; they also help kids build a sense of togetherness, develop empathy, and treat everyone with respect.

It's also important to model the behaviors you wish to instill in your children. Being patient and understanding, and developing excellent problem-solving skills, sets a great example for them to learn from. Kids watch what grown-ups do and imitate it, absorbing the values and ideas we show them. Demonstrating to them how to communicate respectfully and work together creates a positive environment where they feel valued and respected.

The Power of Connection: Building Trust and Understanding

The key to effectively disciplining children is building an emotional connection with them. When you develop a strong bond with your kids, you create a safe and supportive environment where they feel loved and appreciated. This emotional connection allows you to guide them more effectively and decreases the need for punishment.

Building emotional connections with children is not just about showing love, but also about understanding their needs and emotions. Research shows that a strong, secure connection between parents and children can help kids develop the confidence to effectively navigate the world around them (Nivison et al., 2023). Knowing they have a safe and supportive relationship to fall back on can help children feel secure as they explore new experiences. This emotional bond serves as the foundation for implementing effective discipline techniques and fostering positive social and emotional development in children.

Trust-Building Techniques

Trust is key to building any relationship. It lays the foundation for creating a safe and open environment for communication, especially for children. Let's look at a few trust-building techniques you can use to build a healthier relationship with your kids.

Practice Active Listening

One way to build trust is through active listening. When you actively listen to your children without judging or interrupting, it shows that you value their thoughts and feelings. This helps children feel safe and comfortable expressing themselves, leading to a relationship built on mutual respect. For example, when your child is frustrated, responding with empathy to their emotions instead of simply telling them to calm down shows that you care about their feelings, which can further deepen your bond.

To practice active listening:

1. First, give your child your full attention by looking at them when they speak, allowing them to express themselves.

2. Secondly, try repeating what they said in your own words to show you understand.

3. Thirdly, let your child finish speaking without interrupting them.

4. And finally, validate their feelings.

Active listening encourages open communication, helping kids feel more at ease sharing their thoughts and feelings.

Practice Effective Communication

Creating an environment for open and honest conversation allows children to freely express their thoughts and emotions. Taking the time to talk regularly, whether it's during meals or at bedtime, is a great way to keep communication flowing. To practice effective communication, try using "I" statements instead of "You" statements. For instance, saying, "I feel worried when you don't come home on time" is less confrontational and more empathetic than saying, 'You never listen." This subtle shift in language creates a more cooperative atmosphere and lessens defensiveness. Additionally, involving children in discussions about rules and consequences makes it easier for them to understand and accept discipline. When children feel heard and respected, they are more likely to cooperate and adhere to rules.

Pay Attention to Your Children's Needs

Paying attention to your kid's behavior patterns can help you understand their needs. By taking note of situations that lead to positive or negative reactions, you can adjust your approach accordingly. Discuss these patterns with your kids to help them become more self-aware and work together to find solutions. Encouraging self-reflection by asking questions like "How did that make you feel?" or "What do you think could make this situation better?" can help children better understand their emotions and communicate their needs.

Set Communication Guidelines

Setting communication guidelines helps you understand each other. By establishing a regular family meeting schedule, you can share your thoughts and feelings in a safe and open environment. Choosing specific topics to talk about and giving everyone a chance to speak helps create a fair and inclusive home atmosphere. It's also important to agree on some ground rules for communication, like respecting each other's opinions and not interrupting. These simple steps can improve your communication skills and prevent misunderstandings.

Principles of Heart-Centered Discipline

Heart-centered discipline is about more than just pointing out when a child has done something wrong. It's about guiding them with love, empathy, and understanding. By focusing on nurturing your kids' feelings and inner world, you can help them grow into confident and kind individuals. Instead of using fear or punishment to get children to behave, heart-centered discipline encourages accountability and respect. It focuses on teaching children how to be responsible while also ensuring that they feel loved and supported along the way.

Let's look at some key principles of heart-centered discipline.

Empathy

Empathy is essential when it comes to understanding and connecting with kids. It means putting yourself in their shoes and seeing things from their point of view. By showing empathy, you're letting them know that you understand and value their feelings. For instance, when a child is upset, empathy allows you to recognize the reasons behind their behavior, such as frustration or sadness. To show empathy when your child is upset because their favorite toy broke, you could say something like, "I see that you're upset because your toy broke. That must be frustrating." Acknowledging and validating their feelings creates a safe environment for them to express themselves.

Respectful Communication

When you talk to kids respectfully, you help build trust and teamwork. Effective communication involves listening attentively, responding thoughtfully, and avoiding dismissive language. It's about treating children as individuals with valid thoughts and feelings. For example, instead of saying, "Go to bed now," you could say something like, "Hey, it's time to get ready for bed. How about we read a story together?" This approach communicates expectations clearly and shows that you value and respect their feelings and choices. This respectful approach helps you connect better and understand each other's perspective, making disciplinary actions easier to accept and agree upon.

Autonomy

Encouraging kids to be independent is important. Involving children in decision-making teaches them to take accountability for their choices, helping them feel more motivated and disciplined. For instance, you can work together to create household rules or decide on consequences for certain actions. By asking for their input, such as saying, "What do you think should happen if you don't do your chores?" you allow kids to have a say in what happens. This collaboration helps kids develop their decision-making skills and builds their confidence.

Celebrating Growth and Progress

Celebrating growth and progress is crucial in creating a positive learning environment. Recognizing and acknowledging children's efforts, no matter how small, builds their self-esteem and encourages them to keep learning. When your child accomplishes something they have been working on, give them specific and genuine compliments and praise, focusing on the effort they made rather than the outcome. Instead of saying, "Good job," a more effective acknowledgment would be, "I noticed how carefully you painted within the lines. Your hard work really paid off!" Comments like these show how important it is to keep trying and not give up. When you encourage your kids' efforts, however minor the associated accomplishment may seem, it helps them develop a positive attitude toward challenges and setbacks. This can help them build resilience and face obstacles with confidence in the future.

Implementing Heart-Centered Discipline Principles

Implementing heart-centered discipline begins with seeing discipline as a pathway to nurturing growth, understanding, and emotional well-being. By grounding discipline in love, patience, and consistent communication, you create an environment where your children feel safe to express themselves, learn from their mistakes, and thrive. When you show compassion in your daily interactions, you help your kids understand emotions—a crucial part of developing emotional intelligence. This principle is not just about using empathy when disciplining your kids; it's about opening up about your feelings and reactions to show them that it's okay to express emotions. For example, sharing a story about feeling frustrated and how you dealt with it gives your children a real-life example of how to manage emotions. And, over time, they'll learn to manage their own feelings effectively.

Respectful Communication

Respectful communication requires consistency and patience. When disagreements arise, staying calm and speaking clearly can help keep things respectful. By honoring your children's viewpoints, you pave the way for more meaningful connections. For instance, if you disagree over screen time, you could explain your reasons for setting limits while also taking the time to listen to their perspective. Statements like "I understand you want more time to play your game, but too much screen time affects your sleep. Let's find a balance" help them understand the importance of respecting boundaries. This approach allows you to resolve conflicts constructively and teaches children valuable negotiation and problem-solving skills.

Encouraging Autonomy

Encouraging autonomy involves giving kids more responsibility over time, with your help and support. You can start by having them do simple chores and then add on more complex tasks as they get older. This method, called scaffolding, gives children the support they need to become more independent without feeling overwhelmed. For example, younger kids could start by setting the table with some guidance and eventually move on to making easy meals. Each accomplishment helps them gain more confidence and independence. Giving kids choices and letting them deal with the results is a great way to teach them important lessons. When children see the effects of their actions, they learn to take responsibility for their decisions without even realizing it.

Celebrating growth should involve acknowledging the effort that goes into overcoming a challenge. Kids learn best when they're not afraid to make mistakes and when they receive constructive feedback. Instead of focusing on what went wrong, it's important to acknowledge their effort and highlight how they can improve.

Embracing the Discipline With Heart Principles

The discipline with heart principles recognize that neither parent nor child is perfect. It's about progress, not perfection. You see mistakes as opportunities for growth and meet setbacks with understanding, not judgment. This allows you and your kids to embrace vulnerability, cultivating a safe space for learning and growth.

By adhering to these principles, you nurture well-behaved, emotionally intelligent, resilient, and compassionate kids. By implementing the discipline with heart principles, you'll transform discipline from a source of fear and frustration into a journey of mutual learning and connection, helping your family cultivate a relationship rooted in love and trust.

Part II:

The Discipline Spectrum

Chapter 3:
Gentle Guidance—Exploring Soft-Touch Strategies

Each day of our lives we make deposits in the memory banks of our children. –
Charles R. Swindoll

Imagine a child learning to walk. Each stumble is met with patient hands guiding them back to balance—not through force but with gentle encouragement. What if we could approach all aspects of parenting this way, offering support, guidance, and boundaries through the soft touch of understanding rather than rigid control?

Gentle guidance is not about being permissive but about fostering resilience, trust, and emotional intelligence in children. By replacing power struggles with connection and using soft-touch strategies like active listening, compassionate correction, and modeling good behavior, you can nurture your children's growth while preserving joy and peace within your family.

Empathy plays a crucial role in the way we interact with our kids. Listening to your children's emotions and understanding the context behind them creates a loving and supportive environment. By being empathetic, you not only make your kids feel secure and valued but also promote open communication and emotional expression. This helps them feel less afraid and supports them to build a trusting relationship with you.

The Role of Empathy and Understanding

Parenting requires us to momentarily set aside our adult lens and view the world through the eyes of our children. This requires empathy and understanding. What may appear to be stubbornness or disobedience could, in reality, be confusion, frustration, or a cry for attention. Children often act out because they lack the tools to express their emotions appropriately. Tuning into their emotional states allows you to respond with understanding rather than punishment. For instance, when a child throws a tantrum because they don't want to leave the park, it's tempting to interpret this as defiance. But empathy allows you to pause and think about what's beneath the surface. Maybe they're not just resisting your command; they might be sad because they were having fun or overwhelmed by the sudden change. When you approach such situations empathetically, you can guide your kids with calm assurance instead of escalating conflicts.

In practice, gentle guidance with empathy looks like kneeling down to the child's eye level, using a soft voice, and validating their feelings: "I know you're upset because we have to leave, and it's hard to stop playing. How about we say goodbye to the park, and when we get home, we'll do something fun too?" Acknowledging their emotions helps them learn to regulate their feelings while also teaching respect for boundaries.

Empathy doesn't mean you give in to every whim; it means you recognize that behind every behavior is a feeling, and behind every feeling is a need. By addressing those underlying needs with patience, understanding, and gentle correction, you can cultivate emotional intelligence in your children, teaching them to handle life's challenges with grace and resilience.

Strategies for Cultivating Empathy

Empathy is the cornerstone of meaningful and compassionate parenting. It allows us to see the world through our children's eyes, offering us a deeper understanding of their emotions, behaviors, and needs. Cultivating empathy in parenting isn't just about being kind or patient—it's about building connections and helping your kids feel seen, heard, and valued. By intentionally practicing empathy, you teach your children how to recognize and respect the feelings of others, laying the foundation for emotional intelligence and healthier relationships.

Let's explore some practical strategies to help you integrate empathy into your parenting approach, creating a more nurturing and supportive family dynamic.

Practice Active Listening

One way you can practice empathy is by engaging in active listening. In Chapter 1, we briefly talked about the role of active listening in building trust in a parent–child relationship. Active listening involves giving your full attention to your child, maintaining eye contact, nodding, and using verbal cues to show understanding. For instance, when your child expresses frustration about a school situation, you could respond with, "I hear you're upset about what happened at school today. Can you tell me more about it?" This approach will uncover underlying issues that may be affecting your child's behavior—perhaps they're struggling with a particular subject or facing social challenges. When you take the time to really comprehend the reasons behind their actions, you can work on finding a solution instead of just dealing with the issue at the surface level.

Active listening is a great way to make your child feel heard and valued. When you listen attentively to what they are saying, they feel respected and validated, thereby building trust in your relationship.

Understanding Context

Understanding what's going on in your child's life is key to strengthening your bond. Different factors influence a child's behavior; these include their age, external stressors, and their unique personality traits. Recognizing these factors can help you respond to your kids in a way that fits the situation. For instance, dealing with a toddler tantrum caused by the inability to communicate well is different from handling a teenager's rebellious behavior that's driven by a need for independence. An empathetic approach involves seeing the world through your child's eyes and acknowledging their unique experiences and struggles.

Model Openly Sharing Your Feelings

Openly sharing your feelings is another significant aspect of building a culture of empathy. When you're open about your emotions, your children learn that it's safe and normal to express their own emotions. Creating regular opportunities for everyone to share their feelings, whether during dinner conversations or family meetings, creates an environment where emotional honesty is valued. As an example, you might say, "I felt stressed at work today and it helped to talk about it with you." This openness sets an example, encouraging your children to communicate their emotions freely and trust that they will be met with understanding rather than judgment.

Additionally, when kids are encouraged to talk about their feelings, they develop a heightened sense of emotional awareness. This prevents arguments before they start. For instance, when your child says they're stressed about homework, stepping in and offering help or breaking the work down into smaller chunks can help ease the workload. This way, you won't mistake their struggles for laziness or defiance.

Empathy also plays a key role in moments when you need to be firm with your children. Instead of seeing discipline as punishment, empathetic discipline helps you guide your kids toward better behavior while still recognizing and respecting their emotions. Rather than scolding your child for consistently making a mess, you can gently remind them about the importance of keeping things tidy while also acknowledging that playing with toys is fun.

Creating a culture of emotional awareness in your family can help you build healthier relationships. Openly sharing your feelings encourages understanding and mutual respect, while regularly talking about emotions can help you notice patterns and triggers and develop strategies to manage stress. For example, when your child feels stressed, finding solutions together creates a safe environment conducive to their development.

Nonverbal Communication: The Art of Gentle Guidance

Nonverbal communication plays a crucial role in parenting and guiding children. Nonverbal cues can influence how kids respond to rules and consequences—often more powerfully than verbal instructions. You can harness these subtle signals to guide your kids effectively and compassionately.

Understanding how nonverbal signals work provides you with an invaluable tool for encouraging kids to cooperate and build emotional intelligence. To highlight this, research shows that 93% of how we communicate with each other is through nonverbal cues such as facial expressions, body language, gestures, eye contact, and tone of voice (Karni-Visel et al., 2021). Children can pick up on nonverbal cues from a young age. When you use positive nonverbal signals like eye contact, a gentle touch, or encouraging facial expressions, you show empathy, understanding, and support, creating an environment where your kids are more likely to follow instructions.

The Importance of Using Nonverbal Cues

Children are highly attuned to body language, facial expressions, and tone of voice, absorbing emotional cues from their parents to interpret the world around them. A gentle touch, warm smile, or calm posture can communicate safety, love, and reassurance, even when words fall short. On the other hand, crossed arms, a furrowed brow, or a harsh tone can signal frustration or anger, creating anxiety in children. Being aware of your nonverbal communication reinforces empathy, support, and connection, leading to more meaningful interactions with your kids.

Here's how to practice using positive nonverbal cues:

- **Create a supportive atmosphere:** For instance, smiling and nodding while listening to your child shows that you're paying attention and approve of what they're saying. This not only promotes positive interaction but also helps them feel valued and understood. Using supportive body language can help your kids feel more secure, which in turn means they will be less likely to be stubborn or resistant. This makes it easier for them to cooperate and follow rules.

- **Practice mirroring:** Mirroring involves subtly imitating your child's body language, expressions, or gestures. This technique shows your child that you are attuned to their feelings. By mirroring their posture or expressions during a conversation, you can create a sense of rapport and shared experience. This connection can lead to better communication and understanding, making it easier to guide your kids compassionately. Using mirroring in your daily interactions can be simple yet effective. For example, if your child is upset and crossing their arms, you could start by mirroring this posture. Then, gradually shift to a more open stance to encourage them to do the same. This simple cue can make them feel understood and more comfortable to open up emotionally, leading to more productive conversations about whatever is bothering them.

- **Identify and reduce unintentional negative nonverbal cues:** Sometimes unconscious actions, like frowning or crossing your arms, can send a negative message, even if your words are meant to be positive. It's important to be mindful of these nonverbal cues and minimize them. By consciously using positive body language, such as a relaxed posture, a gentle tone, and maintaining eye contact, you can improve your communication with your kids and influence how they perceive and respond to guidance. This simple shift in behavior can make a huge difference in how they receive your messages.

Understanding body language plays a vital role in guiding your children effectively. Being attentive to their nonverbal cues allows you to respond appropriately to their emotional states and needs. For instance, if your child looks sad or is slouching with their eyes down, it could be a sign that they feel discouraged. By being aware of these cues, you can address their emotions instead of just their actions. This kind of understanding can lead to better conversations and deeper connections with your children, helping you guide them more effectively.

Positive Reinforcement Techniques

Using positive reinforcement can help you shape and nurture your kids' behaviors. This approach doesn't just motivate them to keep up the good behavior; it also sets a strong foundation for positive discipline in the future.

Encouraging good behavior is about rewarding the actions you want to see more of. When you acknowledge and reward your child's positive behavior, it motivates them to keep it up. Instead of focusing on punitive measures that discourage undesirable behavior, positive reinforcement creates an environment where good behavior is celebrated and encouraged.

Here are a few strategies to implement positive reinforcement effectively:

- **Reward good behavior:** Rewards can be split into two main groups: tangible and intangible. Tangible rewards are things you can hold, do, or have, like stickers, toys, or extra time using screens. Intangible rewards are more about feelings, like praise, hugs, and uplifting words. The type of reward you use depends on the child's age, their personality, and what they like. For example, younger kids might love getting stickers on a chart, while older kids might prefer something different. It's all about finding what works best for each child to keep them motivated.

- **Establish realistic expectations for desired behavior:** When kids know exactly what's expected of them and what they'll get in return for meeting those expectations, it makes it easier for them to understand and work toward their goals. Unattainable goals can lead to frustration, leading children to want to give up. In contrast, setting realistic and achievable goals instills a sense of accomplishment and motivates them to keep trying. For instance, if you want your child to start cleaning up their toys after playtime, you can gradually build up from them putting away one type of toy at a time to them cleaning the entire play area. Setting small, manageable tasks makes it easier for kids to make lasting changes in their behavior without feeling too pressured or overwhelmed.

- **Understand how positive reinforcement works without manipulating behavior:** It's important to use positive reinforcement in a way that promotes genuine behavior rather than creating a reliance on rewards. For example, cheering on a child for finishing their homework is great, but giving them a treat every time could make them expect a reward for everything. It's important to balance praise with helping them find joy in the task itself. This way, they'll learn to appreciate the value of the behavior and be motivated to do it for their sense of fulfillment.

- **Focus on the positive traits and behavior to encourage good behavior:** Positive reinforcement works best when it highlights a person's strengths and favorable attributes (Morin, 2024). For instance, when you praise your child for their kindness toward others, it reinforces empathy and cooperation. By focusing on and encouraging these behaviors, you help shape their character and nurture a growth mindset.

- **Be flexible in your parenting approach:** There are many ways to encourage children, offering you different options for motivating them. Simple gestures like clapping, cheering, or giving a thumbs-up can greatly increase a child's drive. These nonmaterial forms of reinforcement are not only affordable but also highly impactful in shaping behavior. Alternatively, giving children privileges like extra playtime or special treats can also be effective motivators. To make positive reinforcement effective, consider which approach will resonate best with your child in each situation.

- **Consider the consistency of your reinforcement strategy:** Just as employees expect to be paid regularly and recognized for their hard work, children need consistent reinforcement to learn and understand desired behaviors. If positive reinforcement is given sporadically or inconsistently, it becomes less effective over time. Consistency shows children that their good behavior is noticed and valued, which helps build trust and reliability.

To maintain balance, it's important not to over-rely on rewards. While praising and rewarding good behavior is valuable, children shouldn't expect a treat or prize every time they do something right. A more effective approach is to combine rewards with other parenting techniques, like helping them experience the satisfaction of completing a task or being kind simply for its own sake. This teaches them to appreciate the value of their actions, not just the rewards.

Remember, as kids grow, their needs evolve as well. Adjust your strategies to fit those changing needs. Always be aware of their progress and be willing to adapt your tactics when necessary. Additionally, focus on praising effort and improvement rather than just perfection to encourage ongoing growth. Even small successes should be recognized and rewarded to motivate kids to keep moving forward. For example, if your child begins practicing piano but struggles initially, acknowledging their effort and persistence rather than focusing solely on a flawless performance can cultivate a growth mindset. By doing this, you teach your kids the value of persistence and continuous improvement, laying a foundation for long-term positive behaviors.

Gentle Guidance in Action

Gentle guidance offers a powerful yet compassionate approach to parenting, emphasizing the importance of connection over control and empathy over punishment. By incorporating soft-touch strategies like active listening, nonverbal cues, and gentle correction, you can cultivate emotional intelligence, resilience, and trust in your children. This doesn't mean avoiding discipline; instead, it redefines discipline as a tool for teaching rather than punishing. Through empathy, patience, and a nurturing presence, you guide your children toward growth, helping them navigate challenges confidently.

Empathetic discipline techniques create a positive and understanding atmosphere at home. An empathetic approach allows you to understand the reasons behind your kids' behavior and connect with their emotions, leading to smoother interactions and less fear of criticism. Ultimately, gentle guidance techniques empower you to build a deeper, more harmonious relationship rooted in love, understanding, and mutual respect.

Chapter 4:
Firm Boundaries—Establishing Limits With Love

Encourage your child to think for himself, disagree, and talk about his feelings while accepting your authority. –Henry Cloud

When Sarah noticed that her daughter Katie kept extending bedtime every night, she felt annoyed. At first, it was just a few extra minutes of reading, then it turned into needing a drink or using the bathroom. Before she knew it, bedtime had become a two-hour ordeal. Sarah realized that the problem wasn't just bedtime battles but a lack of clear boundaries.

Parenting requires a delicate balance between nurturing your kids' growth and ensuring they understand the importance of boundaries. Just like Katie, all kids test limits to learn about their environment. Without consistent rules, it's hard for them to understand what's expected of them. Setting clear boundaries can help make bedtime (and other routines) go more smoothly.

Firm boundaries provide structure, safety, and guidance; however, they don't need to come at the expense of warmth or love. When you set limits with care and compassion, your children will not only learn responsibility and self-discipline but also develop a sense of security, knowing that their world is predictable and safe.

The Importance of Consistency and Clarity

Children thrive when they follow a routine and know what to expect. When there's consistency, kids feel safe and secure. Establishing well-defined boundaries leads to clarity, so children are less likely to feel anxious or uncertain about their environment. For example, knowing that bedtime is at 8:00 p.m. every night helps a child settle into a routine, which promotes better sleep and overall well-being.

Responding consistently and predictably builds trust and strengthens your bond. If your child often throws tantrums at the grocery store, remaining calm and taking them outside for a break every time this happens teaches them that you'll handle their emotions calmly and support them.

To minimize misunderstandings and frustration, always be clear about your boundaries. Clarity involves explaining the reasons behind those boundaries. When children understand the "why" behind a rule, they are more likely to internalize it as meaningful rather than arbitrary. For instance, explaining that bedtime is set at a particular hour to help them get enough rest for a fun and productive day tomorrow makes the boundary feel like it's in their best interest, not just a rule imposed by authority. This clarity, combined with consistency, creates a supportive structure within which children can grow confidently, knowing what's expected of them and why.

Here are a few guidelines for effectively communicating boundaries:

- **Use simple, age-appropriate language:** When communicating rules, it's important to use language kids can easily understand. For younger children, keep instructions short and direct. For example, rather than saying, "You need to follow the safety protocol at the playground," you could say, "We need to hold hands when crossing the street." As children grow older, you can expand your explanations, like saying, "We hold hands to stay safe because cars might not see us."

- **Reinforce the rules regularly:** Reinforcing rules should be done with consistent reminders, especially when entering situations where they apply. For instance, before going to the grocery store, a simple reminder like "Remember, we aren't buying toys today. Let's focus on getting the food we need" prepares your child for what to expect and reinforces your boundaries. Additionally, discussing rules during calm moments can help them sink in more deeply.

- **Validate your child's feelings while explaining the importance of the rules:** Acknowledge your child's emotions when setting or enforcing rules, showing them that their feelings are understood. If your child is upset because they can't have more screen time, you might say, "I know it's frustrating when screen time is over, but we have this rule so your brain can rest and you can have fun doing other activities." This helps them see that the rule is there for a reason and that their feelings are valid, even though the rule remains.

- **Provide consistent examples of the desired behavior:** Children learn from watching their parents and caregivers, so modeling the behavior you expect is key. If the rule is to speak respectfully, be sure you are consistently speaking to your child with the same respect you expect from them. If they raise their voice, calmly saying, "We use kind words and a calm voice when we're upset," and demonstrating this by using a calm voice yourself, shows them what respectful communication looks like in action.

Modeling Consistency

Consistency is one of the most powerful tools in parenting. It sets a clear framework for children, helping them understand your expectations and develop accountability for their actions. When children know what to expect and see the same rules applied consistently, it creates a sense of security and structure. For instance, consistently reminding your kids to clean up after playtime reinforces the importance of responsibility. Over time, they will begin to internalize the lesson that taking care of their belongings is part of their routine, and they will start to follow through on their commitments without needing constant reminders.

But consistency isn't just about enforcing rules; it's also about modeling the behaviors you want to see in your children. Kids are highly observant and tend to mimic the actions and attitudes of the adults around them. If they see you handling stress with patience, for instance, they're more likely to learn emotional regulation by following your lead. Imagine you're running late for an appointment, but instead of losing your cool, you take a few deep breaths and calmly explain the situation. Your child witnesses this calm and respectful approach to a stressful situation, which teaches them that managing emotions is possible even when things don't go as planned.

Children often adopt behaviors by watching how adults act in different situations. If you model consistency in your words and actions, they'll mirror that in their behavior. For instance, if you're consistent about saying "please" and "thank you," your child will naturally pick up on these manners and incorporate them into their everyday interactions. Similarly, by staying consistent with your own emotional regulation, you help your children learn to manage their own feelings with greater ease. They will begin to understand that emotions like frustration or anger are normal but can be managed effectively, just like you do when you go through a difficult time.

It's important to remember that modeling consistency isn't about perfection. As parents, we all make mistakes, but how you handle those moments can also serve as a learning experience for your kids. If you lose your temper, calmly apologizing and explaining why it happened shows them that everyone makes mistakes and can learn from them. Consistently demonstrating accountability, even when you're at fault, teaches kids valuable lessons in owning up to their actions and being responsible for how they affect others.

When children grow up in an environment where consistency is modeled, whether in discipline, emotional regulation, or everyday routines, they're more likely to develop the ability to set expectations for themselves, understand accountability, and manage their emotions. They learn that consistency leads to stability and that, with a steady approach, challenges can be overcome with patience and resilience.

Reinforcing Boundaries

Reinforcing boundaries teaches kids how to handle disappointments and challenges in a healthy, positive way. It also instills an understanding of limits and helps them easily adapt. I remember when I set a rule that screen time would end at 7:00 p.m., my son would often protest, hoping for "just five more minutes." The first few nights were tough, with some whining and resistance. But by consistently sticking to the rule, something changed. Eventually, he began to understand the routine and, instead of fighting it, he would turn off the screen without complaint, sometimes even choosing to read a book or play a board game afterward. This simple rule reinforced the idea that boundaries are part of life. Learning to cope with small disappointments helped him build resilience and approach challenges with a more positive mindset, which has served him well—not just at home but at school as well.

Not only is setting boundaries for children important for dealing with their immediate behavior, but it also helps shape their development in the long run. Boundaries give kids a sense of structure and safety as they learn to assert their independence. By making choices within these boundaries, they start to understand the impact of their actions. This early exposure to setting and respecting boundaries improves their ability to handle personal and professional relationships later in life.

Remember, striking a balance between being firm and being flexible is key to effectively setting and reinforcing boundaries. Consistency is important, but sometimes it's okay to make exceptions to accommodate your kids' feelings and unique circumstances. For example, if your child has had a rough day at school, allowing them some extra playtime can show compassion while still keeping a sense of structure overall.

Communication remains a cornerstone in the process of setting boundaries. Explaining the reasons behind the rules helps children understand their importance and encourages compliance.

By setting clear rules with love, you can help your kids develop strong behavioral and emotional skills. In other words, your children will not only learn how to act appropriately now but also develop the tools they need to succeed in the future. Firm boundaries, set with love, can help children feel safe, supported, and ready to handle whatever challenges come their way.

Setting Clear House Rules

Developing and implementing effective house rules that reflect your family values and priorities is crucial for maintaining a harmonious household. These rules can guide behavior, establish expectations, and ensure that everyone feels respected and valued. Here are some practical guidelines to help you create house rules that work.

Set Rules Collaboratively

One of the most effective ways to ensure children adhere to house rules is to involve them in the rule-setting process. Setting rules together gives kids a sense of ownership and responsibility, making it more likely that they will follow whatever's decided. When you sit down together to discuss what rules are necessary, your children feel their opinions matter and understand why certain rules are in place.

For example, instead of just telling your kids they have to be home by a certain time, try asking them what time they think is fair to come home at night. This way, they get to be involved in the decision-making process and learn to think about safety and being responsible. When you decide on a time, it becomes a rule that you both agree on rather than just something you told them to do. This kind of teamwork builds a sense of respect and cooperation, which is important for ensuring your kids follow the rules in the long run.

Communicate Rules Effectively

How you communicate rules can impact how your kids perceive and follow them. It's important to convey rules positively, highlighting the benefits of following them rather than merely focusing on the restrictions.

The benefits of positive communication are as follows:

- **Highlights the importance of having rules in place:** For example, instead of saying, "No using phones at the dinner table," you could frame the rule more positively by saying,

"Dinner time is our opportunity to connect and talk with each other without distractions." This way, everyone sees the benefit of following the rule, which is quality family time.

- **Encourages kids to adhere to rules:** Instead of seeing rules as limitations, you can present them as opportunities for growth and learning. For example, a rule like "Finish your homework before watching TV" instills discipline and teaches kids to manage their tasks efficiently. This approach not only makes the rule sound less restrictive but also associates it with positive outcomes, such as free time after managing responsibilities.

Regularly Revisit Rules

Families are always changing, especially as kids grow older and have different needs. It's important to discuss family rules every now and then to ensure your boundaries still make sense and work for everyone. You can have these discussions at the beginning of each new school year or after big changes, like moving to a new home. This way, you can review the rules together and make any necessary changes. It's an excellent way to maintain trust and transparency in your family: When your kids see that you can adapt rules to fit the current situation, they feel heard and respected.

As your kids get older and start gaining more freedom, it's important to adjust the rules to fit their maturity level. For instance, a curfew set for a younger child may need to be amended as they grow older. By working together to revise the curfew, you can show that you recognize your child's growing maturity while still prioritizing their safety. This highlights that rules are not strict orders but rather guidelines designed to promote your family's well-being.

Celebrate Adhering to Rules

Acknowledging and celebrating positive behavior motivates kids to keep complying. You don't have to do anything big—just a kind word, a hug, or a small reward can show that you appreciate their effort and cooperation. For example, if your child regularly does their chores without you asking, you could say, "I appreciate how responsible you've been with your chores. It makes a big difference in keeping the house neat." This kind of reinforcement not only makes your child feel good about themselves, but it also shows them the importance of following the rules in your family.

You can appreciate your child's good behavior by giving them occasional rewards in addition to praising them. This could be something like allowing extra screen time, planning a fun outing together, or giving them a small treat. Ensure the reward is something that the child values and is directly related to their good behavior. These special celebrations reinforce your family values and create a positive and supportive home environment.

Balancing Freedom With Responsibility

Finding the right balance between giving your children freedom and teaching them responsibility is key to raising happy and well-adjusted kids. It's important to give kids some independence while also helping them understand the consequences of their actions.

Here are some strategies to balance freedom with responsibility:

- **Encourage autonomy:** Allow your kids to make age-appropriate decisions. Giving kids some freedom within safe boundaries helps them feel more in control of their lives—for example, letting younger children choose a bedtime story. With each small decision they make, children learn that their opinions matter, boosting their confidence and helping them become more independent.

- **Link rewards to responsibilities:** If your child wants to spend extra time playing, having them finish their homework first links rewards to responsibilities, helping them understand that taking responsibility leads to more fun activities. When you consistently explain and enforce this concept, your kids will learn the value of managing their tasks effectively, resulting in more enjoyable experiences.

- **Encourage reflection on the outcomes:** Encouraging children to think about the consequences of their choices helps them understand the importance of responsible behavior and enhances their problem-solving skills. When your child makes a significant decision or mistake, take time to reflect on the outcome together. You can guide them by asking questions like, "What could you have done differently?" or "What did you learn from this experience?" This practice promotes self-awareness and improves their decision-making skills.

Encouraging your kids to be independent and giving them more freedom as they show more responsibility nurtures their growth and helps them develop a balanced approach to life. It fosters confidence, and also encourages them to appreciate the value of their freedom and understand the weight of their responsibilities.

Nurturing Independence While Maintaining Boundaries

Firm boundaries are an essential part of raising confident, respectful children. When established with clarity, consistency, and love, they provide the structure children need to feel secure and understand their limits.

When you maintain consistency in your approach to discipline, your children will feel secure and know what to expect. This nurtures trust and creates stability. Clearly communicating your boundaries and expectations is equally important, and can help reduce misunderstandings and anxiety. Remember, kids thrive in a structured environment where they know what's expected of them. By modeling consistent behavior, you teach your kids valuable lessons in accountability and reliability that they will carry into their interactions with others.

Striking a balance between being firm and being flexible when setting boundaries is key to ensuring those boundaries are effective and compassionate. While maintaining consistency is crucial, being adaptable to your kid's developmental needs and unique circumstances is equally important. Flexibility shows empathy and support, and it helps kids see rules as helpful guidelines instead of strict limitations.

Setting clear boundaries and consistently explaining them to your children addresses both your kids' current behavior and their future development. When boundaries are set with love and explained clearly, they become valuable tools that teach children how to navigate the ups and downs of life with confidence and resilience. With firm yet compassionate guidance, you can help your children thrive, laying the groundwork for lifelong success and harmony in the family.

Chapter 5:

Creative Solutions—Thinking Outside the Box

> *You cannot make people learn. You can only provide the right conditions for learning to happen.* –Vince Gowmon

Parenting is a dynamic journey that requires constant adaptation, patience, and innovation. As children grow, so do the challenges we parents face, from managing toddlers' tantrums to navigating the complex emotions of teenagers. While traditional discipline methods may offer structure, they often fall short when it comes to nurturing a child's individuality, emotional intelligence, and cooperative spirit.

In today's fast-paced and evolving world, it's essential to move beyond rigid, one-size-fits-all approaches to discipline. Creative solutions allow you to connect with your kids in meaningful ways. By encouraging their natural curiosity, imagination, and desire for connection, you can unlock their potential and build a closer relationship with them.

Thinking outside the box can turn potential conflicts into opportunities for growth, cooperation, and understanding. Whether it's turning chores into a fun competition, using storytelling to teach empathy, or creating space that encourages emotional regulation, creative parenting brings discipline and development together in powerful, life-shaping ways.

Let's explore how imaginative strategies can cultivate cooperation and connection while reinforcing important values like responsibility and empathy. By embracing a more flexible and playful approach, you can cultivate a home environment where discipline is not a struggle but a shared journey toward mutual respect and emotional growth.

Engaging Cooperation and Creativity

Creating a positive and open home environment can make a difference in how you deal with conflict. Working with your kids and embracing creativity can help you come up with solutions that work for everyone.

This not only enhances your problem-solving skills but also creates a collaborative environment where your kids feel appreciated and understood.

Here are a few strategies to encourage cooperation and cultivate creativity in children:

- **Show your kids that you value their opinions:** One way to achieve this effectively is to involve them in the rule-making process. When children have a say in creating the rules, they feel valued and know their opinions matter. You can have a discussion during a family meeting to establish rules and consequences for breaking those rules. Allowing your kids to share their thoughts and ideas creates a collaborative environment and helps them learn about communication and compromise.

- **Use storytelling:** Using stories to teach children important values is a great way to help them understand right from wrong without coming across as preachy. Stories have a way of capturing a child's attention and imagination, making the message more memorable. You can create stories that reflect situations your kids may encounter in everyday life; for example, a story about a character who learns the importance of sharing through different experiences can resonate with a child who has trouble sharing toys. These stories shouldn't just show the result but should also highlight the emotional journey and struggles along the way. By using storytelling as a tool, you can effectively instill values in your kids in a fun and engaging way, encouraging them to internalize and emulate positive behaviors.

- **Use creative problem-solving techniques:** One way you can resolve conflicts among children is by introducing creative problem-solving techniques, like brainstorming. This can be a fun and effective way for kids to come up with solutions together. When a conflict arises, you can organize a brainstorming session where everyone gets a chance to share their ideas. The focus should be on generating as many ideas as possible instead of worrying about finding the perfect solution right away. For instance, if sharing screen time is an issue, you could try coming up with some new ideas. You could set up a schedule so everyone knows when it's their turn, or find some fun games that your kids can enjoy playing together. This approach not only encourages creativity but also gives your kids a voice in finding a resolution. Whether it's dealing with sibling rivalry or getting children to do their chores, brainstorming can be a valuable tool for encouraging teamwork and building problem-solving skills.

- **Use visual feedback and rewards:** Using charts and other visuals can show progress and motivate your kids to keep up their positive habits. For example, a behavior chart tracking completed chores or kind acts can be a great tool. Your kids can earn stickers or stars for each milestone they reach, with a reward waiting for them once they achieve their goals. The rewards don't always have to be toys or treats; they can also be special privileges or activities. Using visual aids and rewards can help children see the direct link between their actions and the positive outcomes.

Using these strategies requires time and patience. It involves acknowledging and appreciating your children's hard work, which promotes trust and mutual respect. Additionally, these techniques fit in perfectly with today's parenting trends, which prioritize emotional wellness and positive feedback instead of punishment.

Having some practical guidelines can make a difference in encouraging your kids to work together and come up with creative ideas. When you get them involved in setting rules, ensure that the rules are easy to understand, something they can actually do, and age-appropriate. Also, be adaptable and adjust the rules as needed. When brainstorming, create a safe and welcoming space where everyone feels free to share their ideas without the fear of judgment. It's also important to help your children consider how feasible their ideas are and encourage them to think critically about each one. This will not only improve their decision-making skills but also help them become more practical in their problem-solving approach.

When teaching values using stories, pick themes that your kids can relate to and understand. Encourage them to ask questions and talk about what they've learned from the story. Making storytelling interactive and fun can help children learn important lessons in an engaging way.

Developing Problem-Solving Skills

Developing good problem-solving skills can change the way you handle disagreements in your family. Conflicts are bound to happen, but if you work together to solve them creatively and proactively, you can turn them into learning opportunities. By showing your kids how to handle conflicts positively, you help them learn important skills that will benefit them in the future.

Here are a few ways to effectively teach your kids problem-solving skills.

Teach Your Kids to Identify and Name Their Emotions

One way to help kids learn how to resolve conflicts is by teaching them how to talk about their feelings and come up with solutions. This helps them become more independent, as they will learn to understand and express their emotions. You can set a good example of positive communication by using "I" statements when sharing your feelings and needs. For instance, instead of saying, "You never listen to me," you could say, "I feel frustrated when I'm not heard." This small change in communication focuses on expressing your feelings rather than placing blame, making it easier for your kids to understand and imitate your way of communication.

Additionally, it's important to encourage children to name their emotions. When kids say, "I'm angry because someone took my toy," it helps them identify how they feel and can start them on the path to finding a solution. You can teach your children different words to express their emotions and talk about situations where those feelings might come up. As they get better at recognizing and expressing their emotions, they will learn to regulate their emotions and resolve conflicts constructively.

Practice Role-Playing Scenarios

Role-playing can be a great way for kids to practice how to handle different situations they may encounter in real life. By acting out scenarios, they can try out different responses and see the consequences of their actions in a safe space. This not only helps them develop empathy for others but also gives them useful tools for resolving conflicts.

You can create different role-playing scenarios based on everyday conflicts where your kids can practice handling disagreements. For example, they could act out a scenario where two siblings are fighting over a toy. One child can pretend to be upset while the other experiments with ways to fix the situation, like taking turns or coming up with a compromise. Afterward, you can discuss what worked well and what didn't, encouraging good behavior and showing them how to find better solutions in the future.

To make role-playing sessions more fun for your kids, consider using characters from their favorite television shows or books. Children usually connect more with characters they already know and love, which can help them learn important lessons in a more interesting way. By including familiar characters in role-playing games, you can turn it into a fun activity that also teaches valuable life skills.

Create Mind Mapping Solutions

Using visual aids, such as mind maps, can make the brainstorming process easier when trying to resolve conflicts. Mind mapping is a way to visually show different ideas connected to a central problem. This helps kids see every possible solution and their consequences all at once. This technique can be especially useful for kids who learn best when things are presented visually.

To create a mind map, you'll want to write down the main issue in the middle of a large piece of paper. Let's say the problem is about not sharing toys—that goes in the center. Then, you'll draw branches coming off the main issue to represent different solutions or actions. For instance, one branch can be about "taking turns." Under that branch, you can have sub-branches like "set a timer" and "agree on rules." This helps you visualize all the possible steps or outcomes that could help solve the problem. Mapping everything out this way can organize your children's thoughts, helping them come up with a plan to tackle the issue more effectively.

When working through a problem, encourage your kids to think outside the box and come up with new ideas. The more ideas they have, the better chance of finding a solution. After brainstorming together, take a look at all the ideas on the table and discuss the positives and negatives of each idea. This exercise will help them see the problem from different angles and eventually make a well-informed decision.

Evaluate Choices Together

Working together to evaluate the results of different decisions can help your kids develop effective decision-making skills. This involves talking about the consequences of each choice and reflecting on and learning from past decisions, which will help them make more informed and thoughtful decisions in the future.

Start by presenting a situation where you need to make a decision. Let's say you have a free afternoon, and you can't decide whether to go to the park or stay home and play video games. Think about the benefits of each option. If you go to the park, you'll get some fresh air and exercise, but you might have to deal with unpredictable weather. On the other hand, staying home means you can relax and have fun without worrying about the weather and other elements that might affect you, but you might miss out on the chance to socialize and enjoy nature. The conversation should consider all these factors and their long-term effects.

Encourage your kids to share their thoughts and opinions during this discussion, so they know their opinions matter. This way, they can learn to stand up for what they believe in. It's also helpful to look back on past situations and talk about the lessons you learned from them. This reflective practice reinforces the idea that every decision is an opportunity to grow and improve.

Talking about ethical dilemmas can also improve children's decision-making abilities. For example, you could talk about a situation where you find a lost wallet or witness someone being bullied. Talk about the factors that could influence your kids' decisions, highlighting the importance of empathy, honesty, and responsibility. As they work through difficult theoretical situations, they learn how to think about everyone's interests, not just their own, cultivating a sense of moral integrity.

Incorporating Play Into Discipline

Incorporating play into discipline creates a fun and exciting learning experience for kids while maintaining boundaries. This method helps children positively learn from their errors.

Let's look at a few ways in which you can incorporate play into your discipline approach.

Playful Consequences

One way to teach children right from wrong is by using playful consequences. Instead of resorting to traditional punishments like time-outs or taking away privileges, you can try implementing silly tasks as consequences for misbehavior. For example, if your child behaves badly, instead of punishing them, you could ask them to do something fun and silly—like jumping up and down 10 times or singing a funny song. These playful consequences help children learn from their mistakes in a more lighthearted way while still showing them that their behavior was inappropriate.

When using playful consequences, ensure they are connected to the misbehavior at hand. For instance, if your child makes a mess with their toys, you could turn cleaning up into a game by challenging them to pick up the toys while hopping on one foot. This way, they still learn the lesson but in a more enjoyable way—one that feels like a game rather than punishment. This approach not only teaches kids how to correct their behavior but also makes the experience more engaging and educational.

Games as Teaching Tools

Turning lessons into games is another fun way to encourage active participation and make learning enjoyable. By using educational board games, card games, or digital games, children can practice subjects like math, reading, and problem-solving in a fun and interactive way. You can customize games to suit different age groups and skill levels, making learning more enjoyable for everyone. By incorporating these games into their daily learning routines, not only do children learn essential skills, but it also makes the learning process enjoyable and engaging.

For instance, you can teach kids about financial responsibility by playing games like Monopoly or The Game of Life, which mimic real-life financial choices in a fun and controlled setting. Another way to improve math skills is by playing games like Math Bingo or Sum Swamp. These games make practicing addition, subtraction, and other math skills more enjoyable because they hide the typical learning format within a game. So, by incorporating games into learning, kids can have fun while also developing valuable skills.

Set aside time for games regularly. This will help your children get into a routine and be excited about learning. The important part is to pick games that are both enjoyable and educational to keep them engaged. Consistency is key, so try to stick to a set game time each day or week. This way, your kids know what to expect and can look forward to their learning activities.

Use Imaginative Play

When kids pretend to be different characters and act out scenarios, they develop empathy and learn about following rules. Playing make-believe allows children to try out different roles and situations safely, which can help with their emotional and social development. It also gives them the chance to pretend to be adults and explore how different people see things and what society expects from them.

Role-playing activities, such as pretending to run a grocery store or playing house, can help kids learn how to handle complex interactions and responsibilities. To make these games more engaging, you can give your kids props to use and encourage them to come up with stories. For instance, role-playing a family scene can include tasks like setting the table or taking care of a pretend pet, which encourages responsibility and teamwork.

Another imaginative play activity children can engage in is acting out stories from books, or making up their own. This can help them think about important questions and ethical dilemmas in a safe environment. By pretending to be different characters, they can see things from different perspectives and understand the consequences of their choices in a creative way.

Giving your kids costumes, props, and ample space to play can make their pretend play even more fun. Watching and sometimes joining in with their playtime can help you understand how they think, which can make it easier to help them learn and grow.

Celebrating Milestones Through Play

Celebrating achievements is key to nurturing a joyful home environment. Recognizing and celebrating milestones, no matter how small, reinforces positive behavior and cultivates a sense of accomplishment in children. Celebrations don't have to be extravagant; simple, playful acknowledgments can be equally impactful. For instance:

- When someone accomplishes something big, like completing a challenging puzzle or learning something new, a playful celebration could be a mini dance party to celebrate together. Another fun idea is to make a chart with stickers and little prizes to reward your kids each time they reach a goal. These games keep kids motivated and focused on getting closer to achieving their dreams.

- Family game nights can also be a fun way to celebrate special achievements. If your child does something great, like getting good grades or winning a sports game, setting aside a night to play their favorite games is a great way to show them how proud you are. It's not just a reward for the child but also a chance for the whole family to come together, have fun, and create lasting memories. Sharing the joy of these special moments helps strengthen your family bond.

- Another great way to boost your child's confidence and motivation is by telling stories about their achievements. Whether you're reading a book or making up your own tale, focusing on your child's real successes can make them feel proud and encourage them to keep doing their best.

Incorporating play into discipline and celebrations can create a well-rounded environment for children's development. It's all about finding a balance between setting rules and boundaries and cultivating a loving and supportive atmosphere where they are motivated to explore and improve themselves. By using fun consequences, educational games, creative play, and exciting celebrations, you can create a positive and enriching learning experience for your children. This approach helps prepare them for the challenges they'll face in the future while also boosting their social, emotional, and cognitive skills.

Thinking Outside the Box

Discipline doesn't have to be a battle of wills. By engaging your children's natural creativity and involving them in the process, discipline becomes a shared journey of growth rather than a top-down directive.

Let's look at a few important points to remember:

- Coming up with fun and creative ways to handle discipline and conflicts in the family encourages children to use their imagination.

- Involving kids in setting rules helps them feel more responsible and accountable for their actions, leading them to follow the rules they've agreed upon.

- Sharing stories to teach values can make important lessons more meaningful and easier to remember, while brainstorming sessions offer a great opportunity for everyone to come up with solutions together.

- Visual feedback and rewards can be powerful tools for motivating children. By showing them the direct results of their actions, they understand the connection between what they do and the positive outcomes they receive.

Thinking outside the box can create effective, compassionate, and lasting solutions that not only shape your kids' behavior but also encourage connection and emotional intelligence. You can unlock new ways to guide your children by embracing play, creativity, and cooperation, making discipline a positive force that nurtures your bond and encourages self-awareness.

Part III:

Key Themes in Heart-Centered Discipline

Chapter 6:
Forgiveness and Healing

Forgiveness is not an occasional act, it is a constant attitude. –Martin Luther King Jr.

Forgiveness is one of the most powerful tools for cultivating emotional resilience and harmony in relationships. It helps families move beyond grudges, rebuild trust, and break the cycle of negativity and resentment that can weigh down relationships. Holding onto grudges doesn't just create tension; it can shift the entire dynamic of a household, allowing bitterness and anger to take root. But when we learn to forgive, we give our relationships the chance to heal, creating a fresh start where love and trust can flourish.

I remember one weekend when my kids had a massive fight over who got to sit in the front seat of the car (classic sibling rivalry!). The argument spiraled into a day of silence and cold shoulders. By bedtime, tensions were still high, but instead of lecturing, I sat them down and shared a story from my childhood about a grudge I'd held onto for way too long. They saw how much energy it had taken out of me and how freeing it was to finally let it go. We talked about forgiveness, not just as an act of kindness toward others but as something we do for ourselves.

When you model forgiveness, it sets a powerful example for your kids. It shows them that mistakes are part of life, but what matters most is how they move forward together. This practice doesn't just strengthen family bonds; it teaches your children how to build healthier relationships outside the home too. Through forgiveness, you can restore relationships and create a safe space where love, trust, and growth thrive.

The Role of Forgiveness in Parenting

Forgiveness involves a prosocial motivational shift toward someone who has caused harm (McCullough, 2001). Learning to regulate negative emotions and move toward forgiveness is vital for children's emotional well-being and ability to maintain healthy relationships, especially if they have experienced difficult situations like parental divorce (van der Wal et al., 2024). Teaching kids about forgiveness can help them navigate the complex emotions of anger and resentment and eventually reach a place of peace and reconciliation.

When you model forgiveness, you set a powerful example for your children. Acknowledging mistakes and showing a willingness to move forward together not only deepens your family bond but also influences external relationships. Your kids learn that mistakes are inevitable, but that what matters is how they address those mistakes and work toward repair. This lesson in forgiveness can deeply impact their ability to build empathetic, compassionate relationships, whether with friends, teachers, or peers.

The Benefits of Forgiveness

Forgiveness in parenting offers a wealth of benefits, both for you as a parent and for your children. It plays a vital role in creating a healthy, emotionally resilient family atmosphere where you acknowledge and learn from mistakes and resolve misunderstandings with love and understanding.

Forgiveness has numerous benefits, including the following.

Strengthens the Family Bond

Forgiveness strengthens the relationship between you and your children by creating an environment of trust and emotional safety. When you forgive your kids for their mistakes, you show them unconditional love. This strengthens your bond, and your kids will feel safe enough to come to you with their challenges, knowing they won't be met with harsh judgment but rather with understanding and guidance.

Teaches Accountability and Empathy

When you model forgiveness, your children learn to take responsibility for their actions without fear of rejection or punishment. They understand that while mistakes happen, what matters is owning up to them and working toward repair. Forgiveness also teaches empathy, as children begin to recognize that everyone makes mistakes and deserves understanding, which helps them relate to others with compassion.

Enhances Emotional Resilience and Regulation

Forgiveness helps both parents and children manage difficult emotions like anger, frustration, or disappointment. It encourages emotional regulation and the ability to move forward instead of holding onto grudges or reacting impulsively. When you forgive your child or ask for their forgiveness, you demonstrate how to manage complex emotions healthily, promoting their long-term emotional resilience.

Promotes Positive Conflict Resolution

Conflict is inevitable in any family, but forgiveness shifts the focus from winning an argument to resolving issues in a productive, loving way. By teaching your child how to forgive and seek forgiveness, you equip them with critical skills for conflict resolution. They learn to communicate openly, express their feelings, and find solutions without holding onto resentment.

Reduces Stress and Tension

Holding onto grudges and unresolved anger can create a tense atmosphere in the home. By embracing forgiveness, you let go of negativity and show your kids that peace and harmony are more important than being right. This reduces stress for everyone, and creates a more relaxed, supportive environment where each member of the family feels valued and understood.

Encourages a Growth Mindset

Forgiveness encourages a growth mindset, where you view mistakes as learning opportunities rather than failures. It shows that missteps can be corrected and that it's possible to grow from even the most difficult situations. This empowers children to take risks, knowing that their worth isn't tied to perfection but to their efforts and capacity to learn from their experiences.

Improves Communication

Making forgiveness a central part of your family life improves your communication. Your children will feel safe expressing their emotions, even when they're upset or have done something wrong, because they know that forgiveness is possible. This open dialogue encourages honesty and transparency, reducing the chances of misunderstandings or pent-up frustration.

Models Healthy Relationships

Children look to their parents to understand how relationships should function. By consistently practicing forgiveness, you model what healthy relationships look like—ones that are built on understanding, empathy, and mutual respect. This lesson not only helps your kids navigate family dynamics but also equips them with skills for building strong, loving relationships outside the home.

Promotes a Positive Home Environment

A home that prioritizes forgiveness is one where love and acceptance flourish. Mistakes aren't met with harsh punishment or lingering resentment but with the opportunity to learn, grow, and reconnect. This creates a nurturing space where everyone feels safe to be themselves, enhancing your whole family's emotional and psychological well-being.

Encourages Forgiveness in Future Relationships

Children who grow up in an environment where forgiveness is practiced are more likely to carry this value into their future relationships. They'll have a greater capacity to forgive friends, partners, and colleagues, allowing them to build stronger, more compassionate connections in their personal and professional lives.

Incorporating forgiveness into your parenting allows you to create a supportive, emotionally rich environment where you and your kids can grow. It teaches valuable life lessons about love, resilience, and understanding, helping to shape emotionally healthy, well-rounded individuals.

Teaching Kids About Forgiveness

Integrating regular discussions and rituals around forgiveness into family life is an effective way to teach your kids about the importance of forgiveness. These practices create a safe space for emotional expression and offer opportunities for everyone to address and resolve grievances. Family meetings, for example, can allow you to share your feelings and ask for or offer forgiveness when needed. Additionally, creating a forgiving environment encourages honesty and vulnerability, making everyone feel understood and supported.

Establishing a culture of forgiveness at home lays the groundwork for building emotional resilience in your children, a vital trait that will equip them to handle life's inevitable challenges and conflicts with a balanced, positive approach. For example, while all siblings argue, children raised in a forgiving culture are more likely to resolve their differences constructively, without harboring lingering resentment.

How do you teach your kids to forgive? Let's look at a few strategies you can begin with:

- **Model forgiveness:** Seeing forgiveness in action teaches children to extend the same grace to their peers, cultivating empathy and reducing conflict. Studies show that practicing forgiveness is linked to improved physical and mental health, better conflict-resolution skills, and stronger social support systems (Raj et al., 2016). When children observe their parents resolving disagreements with compassion and understanding, they are more likely to model these behaviors in their interactions with friends and classmates. This ripple effect extends beyond the home, contributing to a more empathetic, cooperative community.

- **Help kids develop their socio-cognitive skills:** Children's ability to forgive is linked to their developing socio-cognitive skills, such as understanding others' thoughts and feelings. As children grow older and develop these abilities, they show a greater capacity to forgive and apologize. In turn, this forms the foundation for effective communication and relationship-building, essential skills for handling social interactions throughout life.

- **Create a forgiving environment at home:** Regular family discussions, where everyone can voice their feelings and seek forgiveness if needed, can reinforce the importance of open communication and collective healing. Implementing rituals such as "forgiveness circles," where each family member shares something they've forgiven, shows the power of coming together to support and understand each other. These practices not only build emotional resilience but also teach kids valuable life skills they will carry into adulthood.

Studies show that forgiveness in children is linked to better mental health, decreased aggression, and stronger interpersonal relationships (Ávila, 2022). Teaching children the value and practice of forgiveness early on helps them develop coping skills and emotional regulation, enabling them to handle stress and conflicts more effectively. These skills are invaluable—especially in school settings, where peer interactions are frequent and diverse.

Additionally, cultivating a forgiving environment at home promotes a culture of empathy and cooperation. When kids learn to forgive, they develop empathy and understand that everyone makes mistakes and deserves a second chance. This makes it less likely for them to react aggressively during conflicts, leading to a more peaceful and friendly environment at home and in the community.

Forgiveness in the family isn't just about getting over past arguments; it's also about preventing future ones. It prepares kids to work through disagreements positively, reducing conflicts and creating a harmonious atmosphere at home.

Steps to Genuine Apologies

One of the most challenging yet profoundly healing practices in family relationships is offering a sincere apology. Apologies, when given with genuine intent, can be a powerful tool for repairing and strengthening relationships.

Let's look at a few steps to guide genuine apologies:

1. **Acknowledge the harm caused by your actions:** When we take responsibility for the pain we've inflicted, we validate the other person's emotions. This validation is crucial, as it helps the other person feel seen and understood and lays a foundation for rebuilding trust. Ignoring or downplaying the impact of your actions can exacerbate the hurt, leading to further emotional distance. To properly acknowledge the hurt, it's important to be specific. For instance, saying, "I realize my words were harsh yesterday, and I know they hurt you deeply" shows that you're aware of the impact of your actions and the emotional consequences.

2. **Express genuine remorse:** A heartfelt apology should come from a place of vulnerability, with a simple yet powerful phrase like "I'm sorry." This act of humility not only demonstrates personal accountability but also models for children the

importance of owning their mistakes. Research shows that when someone apologizes sincerely, it becomes easier for others to respond with empathy, making forgiveness more attainable (Engel, 2002). A statement like "I'm truly sorry for how I acted" can convey this authenticity. Regret must be expressed without excuses or justifications, as these can dilute the sincerity of the apology.

3. **Create actionable steps to make amends:** Offering a concrete plan to address the situation shows not only a commitment to change but also a deeper understanding of the harm caused. This could involve asking the person who has been hurt what they need to feel better, or suggesting specific actions to rectify the situation. For example, if you missed an important event due to work commitments, you could say, "I will make it a point to attend all your future games and events, and I want to make up for missing this one. Let's spend some extra time together this weekend." These actions reinforce your apology by showing a genuine willingness to change and prevent future mistakes.

4. **Maintain open communication:** Encouraging an honest dialogue gives everyone the space to process their emotions and offer forgiveness authentically. Asking questions like "How did my actions make you feel?" or "Is there anything else you want me to understand about how this affected you?" encourages mutual understanding and respect. This back-and-forth exchange helps everyone heal and learn from the experience, reducing the chance of future conflicts.

Research shows that apologies and confessions increase empathy, making it easier for people to forgive (Engel, 2002). This underscores the importance of emotional connection in the apology process. A heartfelt apology can bridge the divide caused by hurtful actions, ultimately strengthening your relationship over time.

Healing From Family Conflict

Understanding and addressing family conflicts requires recognizing recurring patterns and triggers. While each family has its own unique dynamics, certain behaviors often repeat, creating predictable sources of tension. For example, continually arguing over bedtime routines or disagreeing about household chores can be significant points of contention.

Identifying these recurring issues can help you develop proactive strategies to manage expectations and adjust your responses, leading to more effective resolutions. Recognizing and anticipating specific triggers allows you to approach conflicts more calmly and constructively.

Here are a few strategies to handle family conflicts effectively:

- **Embrace vulnerability and maintain open communication:** Expressing feelings honestly and transparently cultivates a deeper understanding within the family. When everyone expresses their emotions and perspectives openly, it models healthy conflict resolution and encourages others to lower their defenses, creating an environment where empathy and compassion can grow. Open communication not only defuses tension but also strengthens emotional bonds, promoting long-term family harmony.

- **Apply targeted conflict resolution techniques:** Active listening, for instance, plays a vital role in validating emotions and reducing defensiveness. By fully focusing on what the other person is saying and acknowledging their feelings without judgment or interruption, everyone feels heard and respected, leading to better understanding. Additionally, using "I" statements—such as "I feel hurt when…"—instead of accusatory language such as "You always…" shifts the focus from accusing the other person to expressing your emotions, encouraging more empathetic, solution-focused conversations.

- **Embrace the post-conflict healing process:** After resolving a conflict, it's helpful to hold debriefing sessions where you discuss what happened and how you addressed the issue. These conversations give you time to reflect on what worked well and where you need to improve. Following up with bonding activities, like family outings or game nights, is a great way to bring you closer together and ensure positive experiences overshadow moments of discord. Celebrate the fact that you managed to put aside your differences, no matter how insignificant this may seem. This will help you recognize that overcoming conflicts as a family is an achievement worth celebrating.

- **Establish regular family meetings where you can address concerns before they escalate into major conflicts:** During these meetings, everyone has a chance to voice their thoughts and propose solutions. This proactive approach keeps communication flowing and minimizes the risk of simmering tensions. Additionally, maintaining a conflict journal can help you identify recurring issues and provide insights into patterns and triggers.

- **Engage in empathy-building exercises:** Empathy plays a critical role in resolving conflicts by enabling you to understand each other's perspectives. Simple activities like sharing daily highs and lows can promote empathy by allowing each person to connect with the others' emotional experiences. These exercises not only promote a culture of understanding but also make it easier to deal with future conflicts compassionately and respectfully.

Incorporating trust-building activities into your family routine can greatly enhance post-conflict healing. Conflicts can diminish trust, and one of the most effective ways to rebuild trust is through consistent actions and open communication. Exercises like the "trust fall," where one person falls back and relies on another to catch them, serve as a metaphor for letting go of control and placing confidence in each other. Similarly, "rose and thorn sessions," where everyone shares a positive and a challenging moment from their day, encourage openness and help strengthen trust.

Finally, celebrating resolutions is a simple yet powerful way to strengthen positive conflict management. After resolving a disagreement, take a moment to recognize everyone's cooperation and effort. This could be as simple as acknowledging each other's contributions or sharing a special meal. These celebrations provide positive reinforcement, making it more likely that everyone will continue to use constructive conflict-resolution strategies in the future.

Modeling Forgiveness

Embracing the transformative power of forgiveness can be a game-changer in family relationships. Forgiveness is more than just a way to resolve conflicts; it's a tool for rebuilding trust, breaking free from cycles of resentment, and creating an environment where love, support, and emotional growth flourish. When you let go of grudges and past hurts, you open the door to healing and harmony, allowing everyone in the family to feel valued and understood.

By modeling forgiveness, you teach your kids some of the most important life lessons: empathy, compassion, and the ability to resolve conflicts with grace. These lessons extend far beyond the family, shaping how children interact with friends, classmates, and, eventually, their own partners and children. Incorporating regular discussions and rituals around forgiveness can strengthen these bonds, making your home a safe haven for emotional expression and healing.

In the end, a family grounded in forgiveness isn't just better equipped to handle life's challenges—it's also stronger, more united, and filled with love that stands the test of time.

Chapter 7:
Celebrating the Positive

The bond that links your true family is not one of blood, but of respect and joy in each other's life. –Richard Bach

Celebrating positive behaviors at home creates a nurturing and joyful environment where everyone feels appreciated. Reinforcing these actions not only contributes to the overall atmosphere but also ensures each family member feels valued and motivated. For example, when your kids tidy up their rooms without being asked, rather than just thanking them, highlight how thoughtful it was that they took the initiative to keep the space tidy. Saying something like, "You did that all on your own, and it really helped me today" makes a world of a difference.

When we focus on the good, we shift children's perspective and help them understand the value of their actions. This specific recognition builds their sense of self-worth, motivating them to continue these positive behaviors. Over time, it also encourages an environment rooted in trust, appreciation, and a shared desire to contribute positively to the household.

Focusing on the good affects not only your child but also the overall dynamic in your household. When children see their positive actions being celebrated, they start to connect their behavior with the joy it brings to others, motivating them to keep it up. Over time, this builds trust, mutual respect, and a shared commitment to maintaining a happy, supportive home. By celebrating everyday moments and milestones, you create a space where kindness, initiative, and thoughtfulness are the norm, and where each family member feels inspired to be their best self.

Shifting Focus: Recognizing and Reinforcing Positive Behaviors

In any home, acknowledging positive behaviors creates an uplifting and encouraging atmosphere. When you focus on reinforcing desired actions by genuinely praising your kids for their efforts, you set the stage for a joyful and trusting environment where they feel valued and motivated.

To reinforce positive behavior in kids, try the following strategies:

- **Offer genuine praise:** Genuine praise can significantly encourage the behaviors you wish to see more of in your children. Simply saying, "Good job!" isn't enough for praise to resonate; it must be specific and heartfelt. General compliments like "Well done" lack the detail needed for children to understand exactly what they did well. Instead, specific praise, such as saying, "I really appreciate how you cleaned up your toys without being asked," provides clear, actionable feedback that reinforces the precise behavior you wish to see repeated. This helps children understand the value of their actions and encourages them to continue exhibiting such behaviors.

- **Focus on positive behaviors rather than mistakes:** Human nature often draws attention to mistakes and misbehavior, but constantly pointing out faults can lead kids to seek attention through negative actions. By celebrating positive behaviors instead, you can shift your children's focus toward repeating those desirable actions. For example, if a child habitually forgets to put away their shoes but one day remembers without prompting, praising this specific action can encourage them to make it a habit. This approach reduces the need for negative attention-seeking and encourages an environment of trust and value. Children who feel valued for their positive efforts develop a stronger sense of self-worth and are more likely to cooperate and contribute positively to the household.

- **Regularly highlight achievements, no matter how small:** This serves as a constant source of motivation. Success, whether big or small, should never go unnoticed. Acknowledging even small achievements, whether it's finishing homework on time or helping with household chores, instills a sense of accomplishment and promotes a positive mindset. This consistent affirmation builds resilience and confidence in children, teaching them to appreciate progress over perfection.

Strategies for Reinforcing Positive Behavior

Reinforcing positive behavior in children creates a nurturing environment where they can flourish emotionally and socially. By emphasizing encouragement and recognition, you can guide their actions in impactful ways, helping them develop confidence and empowering them to make constructive choices.

Let's look at a few strategies to encourage good behavior in kids.

Family Meetings

Family meetings provide an opportunity to celebrate your achievements and reinforce positive values. Use family meetings as special occasions where you recognize and celebrate each other's accomplishments. This allows children to feel valued, enhancing your family bond and helping them recognize each other's efforts. For example, a weekly family meeting could include a segment where everyone shares something positive they observed another family member doing. This practice not only highlights individual achievements but also cultivates mutual respect and affection among siblings.

Ensure that you get your kids involved in these discussions. This will help them understand the value of acknowledging each other's efforts and contributions, reinforcing a culture of gratitude and celebration within your family.

Value Effort Rather Than the Outcome

Additionally, using positive reinforcement to praise effort and improvement, rather than focusing solely on perfect outcomes, can have a profound impact on your child's growth mindset and resilience. When children know that their hard work is valued regardless of the result, they become more motivated to try new things and persist through challenges. This helps them embrace mistakes as part of the learning process and understand that progress is more important than perfection.

Provide Immediate Praise

Offering immediate praise when positive behavior begins, rather than waiting for your children to finish a task, can be highly effective. For example, if your kid starts working on a challenging homework assignment, recognizing their effort early on will encourage them to continue. This early reinforcement cultivates a sense of achievement and motivates them to stay focused, knowing that you appreciate their efforts.

Link Rewards to Positive Behavior

In the same way, linking rewards to positive behavior strengthens the connection between desired actions and favorable outcomes. When children see that their positive behavior leads to enjoyable rewards, they are more likely to repeat those actions. For instance, if your child has consistently helped around the house, allowing them to choose a fun family activity for the weekend reinforces the idea that their efforts lead to meaningful rewards.

Consistent positive reinforcement is key to embedding good behaviors as lasting habits. Just as adults expect regular payment for consistent work, children need frequent acknowledgment of their positive actions to stay motivated. This doesn't mean overwhelming them with rewards but rather finding a balanced approach where you recognize their efforts, particularly when they are learning a new behavior. As the behavior becomes more habitual, less frequent reinforcement can maintain the pattern, with occasional rewards providing extra motivation.

It's equally important to avoid unintentionally reinforcing negative behaviors. Sometimes, negative attention, like scolding or arguing, can encourage undesirable actions. For example, if your child notices that misbehaving is the best way to get your attention, they may continue acting out. Ignoring minor misbehaviors and instead focusing on reinforcing positive actions can guide them toward more desirable habits. By focusing more on positive behaviors, you can create a more effective and uplifting system of discipline and encouragement.

Creating a Culture of Gratitude at Home

Practicing gratitude is an effective way to create a joyful and appreciative environment. Incorporating gratitude practices into your family routine can transform the emotional atmosphere at home.

Below are some simple yet effective strategies for cultivating gratitude that can strengthen your family relationships, enhance your kids' emotional intelligence, and help them build resilience.

Create Gratitude Rituals

Introducing daily gratitude rituals doesn't need to be complicated; small acts can make a big difference. For example, each morning, or at dinnertime, take turns sharing one thing you are grateful for. This simple habit cultivates a sense of appreciation and encourages your children to reflect on the positive aspects of their day. It also nurtures emotional intelligence, teaching your kids how to express their feelings and recognize the value of gratitude in their lives.

Have a Gratitude Jar

A gratitude jar is another effective tool to encourage reflection and shared joy. Simply place a jar in a central spot, along with slips of paper and pens, and encourage everyone to write down what they're thankful for. This practice not only reinforces positive thinking but also strengthens your bond by allowing you to celebrate moments of gratitude together. Over time, the jar will become a meaningful collection of cherished memories, providing comfort and perspective during tough times by highlighting life's blessings.

Model Gratitude

When you actively model gratitude, you teach your children to appreciate the positives in life and handle challenges with resilience. Children learn by observing their parents' actions. When you express gratitude, such as thanking your kids for helping with chores or recognizing your partner's effort, you model good behavior. This helps your kids focus on the positive aspects of life, even during difficult times.

Practicing gratitude equips children with tools to reframe negative situations and maintain a hopeful outlook. Research shows that cultivating gratitude can significantly enhance emotional resilience, encouraging children to find silver linings in challenging moments (Housman Institute, 2019).

Have Gratitude-Focused Conversations

Encouraging gratitude-focused conversations in the family can deepen understanding and create a supportive environment. Whether during meals, on walks, or before bed, sharing what each family member is grateful for can cultivate empathy and emotional connection. Consistency and sincerity are key to making these conversations impactful. Involving your kids in this practice teaches them to express their feelings and develop active listening skills. This enhances their emotional intelligence and creates an environment where everyone feels heard, valued, and supported.

Daily Rituals That Promote Joy

Creating daily rituals can cultivate joy and deepen connections within your family. These small, consistent practices bring a sense of routine and togetherness that can uplift everyone's mood and foster a warm, supportive environment. Whether it's starting the day with a shared breakfast, ending the evening with gratitude reflections, or having regular family walks after dinner, these moments create opportunities to bond and share experiences. Rituals like reading together before bedtime or holding weekly family game nights can also spark joy and give everyone something to look forward to. Incorporating these simple habits into your daily routine enhances the home atmosphere and builds lasting memories and a stronger family unit.

Game Nights

Game nights are a fun and engaging way to bond as a family. Setting aside dedicated time each week for playing games together creates opportunities for bonding and joyful interactions. These moments of shared laughter and friendly competition can relieve tension and stress, promoting a deeper connection. Whether it's a board game, a card game, or even charades, playing together cultivates a sense of unity and togetherness.

Regular Family Meals

Family mealtime is equally important. Gathering around the table to share a meal creates a sense of belonging through shared activities. It provides an invaluable opportunity to engage in meaningful conversations, share your experiences, and express your thoughts and feelings. This supports your emotional connection, encourages healthy eating habits, and builds a routine that everyone looks forward to.

Spend Time in the Outdoors

If you love to spend time in nature, scheduling regular outings can help you create lasting memories. Spending time outdoors, whether at a local park, on a hiking trail, or even in your backyard, promotes shared excitement and is a great way to escape the demands of daily life. Nature has a calming effect on the mind and body, and these shared experiences deepen your bonds through adventure and exploration. Take walks together, pack a picnic, participate in outdoor sports, and have fun while connecting.

Celebrate Family Milestones

Celebrating family milestones is a great way to pause and reflect on your journey and acknowledge the blessings in your life. Whether it's celebrating a birthday, a graduation, or a small personal victory, acknowledging these moments with unique traditions deepens your connection, cultivates gratitude, and promotes a supportive home environment.

Rituals don't have to be something extravagant. It could be something as simple as making handmade cards, baking a favorite cake, or planning a special outing. This not only highlights individual accomplishments but also shows that you are proud and supportive of each other.

To celebrate milestones, try the following:

- **Make them part of your family meetings:** These gatherings give you a perfect opportunity to reflect on positive behaviors, honor each other's input, and plan fun or meaningful activities together. When everyone's voice is heard and their contributions acknowledged, it cultivates a sense of belonging and mutual respect, reinforcing the idea that every family member is important.

- **Set aside time each day to acknowledge everyone's efforts:** Another simple yet impactful ritual is setting aside time each day to recognize each other's efforts. For example, during dinner, you can introduce a "highlight of the day" moment where each person shares something positive that happened. This practice shifts the focus to the good, encourages gratitude, and builds a deeper appreciation for each other's experiences. It creates an uplifting atmosphere where everyone is recognized and appreciated.

- **Highlight positive behaviors:** You can also highlight positive behaviors. Whether acknowledging how a child helped with chores or praising a thoughtful gesture, celebrating these actions reinforces good behavior and cultivates a tone of appreciation. It shows kids that their actions matter and helps them understand the ripple effect of kindness and consideration, promoting a family culture where positivity is celebrated and nurtured.

Recognizing Good Behavior

Reinforcing positive behavior isn't just a parenting tool—it's a transformative approach that can improve your emotional well-being. By intentionally recognizing and celebrating your kids' positive behavior, you create a supportive environment where trust thrives. This enhances children's sense of self and strengthens their self-esteem and resilience, setting the stage for more harmonious and connected family relationships.

As we have explored throughout this chapter, methods for reinforcing positive behavior can vary widely, from daily rituals like family game nights and shared meals to more structured celebrations of achievements. Each approach is unique, yet they all share a common goal: to nurture a family environment where children feel seen, valued, and motivated to strive to be their best selves.

Additionally, consistently reinforcing positive behaviors instills important life skills in children, such as empathy, gratitude, and the ability to recognize and express their feelings. By modeling gratitude and maintaining open communication, you not only empower your children but also deepen your familial bond, creating a solid foundation for healthy relationships that can weather life's challenges.

Chapter 8:
Seeking and Offering Support

The most important things in life are the connections you make with others. –Tom Ford

Building a strong support system is one of the most powerful things you can do to enhance your parenting journey and create healthier family relationships. In today's fast-paced world, juggling work, home responsibilities, and your children's needs can feel overwhelming. That's why having a reliable network of people to lean on isn't just helpful—it's essential.

I'll never forget the time when my first child was born. Like so many new parents, I believed I could manage it all on my own; after all, I'd prepared for months. But after countless sleepless nights and feeling like I was barely keeping my head above water, I realized I needed help. Family and friends quickly became my lifeline. Whether it was a quick phone call for advice on baby care or a much-needed offer to babysit so I could take a nap, their support made a world of difference.

That experience taught me an important lesson: Seeking help is not a sign of weakness but a smart, healthy, and essential part of parenting. Trying to do everything on your own can lead to burnout, and when you're exhausted, it's harder to be the parent you want to be. On the other hand, leaning on a network of family, friends, or even other parents can relieve stress, keep you grounded, and provide a fresh perspective on any challenges you're facing.

For instance, a friend of mine once shared how joining a local parenting group transformed her experience as a new mom. Before she found that community, she often felt isolated and overwhelmed, unsure if what she was going through was normal. But connecting with other parents who were facing similar struggles gave her a sense of community and reassurance. They shared tips, watched each other's kids during emergencies, and provided a space where she could vent her frustrations without judgment.

The benefits of having a support system extend beyond just reducing stress; these networks can also help you model healthy relationships for your children. When kids see their parents seeking and accepting help from others, and offering help when someone else needs it, they learn the value of community and that no one has to do everything alone. This teaches them to seek out healthy relationships and build support networks in their own lives as they grow.

Seeking support from others not only makes parenting more manageable but also enhances your family life. It allows you to create more quality time for bonding with your children, supports you to recharge when needed, and gives you the confidence to face parenting challenges with a refreshed and clear mind.

When to Seek Professional Help

Recognizing when to seek professional help is one of the most important aspects of responsible parenting. Many parents feel they must handle everything themselves, but there are times when outside intervention is necessary for your family's well-being. Knowing when to seek professional assistance can make all the difference in managing difficult situations and preventing small issues from escalating into larger problems.

Recognizing Behavioral Concerns

Recognizing when your child's behavior indicates deeper issues is crucial in parenting. Persistent patterns of disruptive behavior—for example, when a child consistently displays aggressive behavior, withdraws from social situations, or has difficulty staying focused—can be an early sign that you need to seek intervention. Monitoring these behaviors and seeking professional help if there's no change is crucial. Consulting a pediatrician or child psychologist can help you identify the underlying causes and appropriate interventions, guiding you toward a healthier family life.

Understanding Emotional Struggles

Taking care of our emotions is just as crucial as taking care of our physical health. If your kids experience prolonged sadness or anxiety, or frequent mood swings, they may need support beyond what you can provide. These emotional challenges can impact their school performance, friendships, and overall happiness. If you notice your child losing interest in activities they once enjoyed, changes in their eating or sleeping habits, or excessive worry, it could be time to reach out for professional help. Early intervention can make a significant difference in their well-being.

Family Dynamics

Strained family relationships can create a toxic environment for children, affecting their emotional development. If conflicts become frequent or are impossible to resolve, family therapy can provide a neutral space where you can express your feelings and learn effective communication techniques. Addressing these issues early can restore harmony and create a more supportive home.

Seeking professional help is not a sign of weakness but a testament to the love you have for your family and your sense of responsibility. Whether it's behavioral challenges, emotional struggles, or relationship difficulties, there are experts available to guide and support you. Reaching out for help, when needed, is a vital part of proactive and effective parenting.

Parental Burnout

Burnout can sneak up on you, especially when you're managing a lot of responsibilities. Signs like emotional exhaustion, irritability, and neglecting self-care are red flags that you might be running on empty. For example, if you find yourself snapping at your kids over something small or feeling constantly overwhelmed, it might be time to address burnout. Seeking support from a therapist or counselor can provide helpful strategies to manage stress, restore balance, and allow you to be more present and engaged with your children.

As parents, we often feel the need to shoulder everything on our own, but seeking support from friends, family, or professional groups can provide valuable outlets for sharing emotions and gaining fresh perspectives. Letting go of some responsibilities and prioritizing self-care is crucial in combating burnout. Simple habits like regular exercise, getting enough sleep, and eating a balanced diet can reduce stress. Additionally, carving out time for activities you enjoy helps you relax and recharge your energy. Practicing self-care promotes a healthier, more rewarding parenting experience.

Building a Support Network: Community Resources and Peer Support

Imagine how different your parenting journey could be with a network of supportive people in your corner. Having a circle of fellow parents, as well as community resources, can make the parenting journey more enjoyable, whether you need emotional support or practical advice. Let's face it, parenting is way easier when you've got a team backing you up!

Let's look at a few strategies to help you build a support network:

- **Identify local resources:** Local parenting classes offer invaluable education and can connect you with other parents facing similar challenges. These classes often cover topics such as child development, discipline strategies, and effective communication. Attending these sessions can give you new insights and help you connect with fellow parents, cultivating a sense of community. Additionally, there are different local community services aimed at assisting parents. Libraries, community centers, and hospitals frequently hold parenting workshops, health checkups, and playgroups for children, which provide opportunities to interact with other parents and share your experiences.

- **Connect with other parents through informal support networks within schools and neighborhoods:** Schools are a great place to network with other parents. Volunteering for school events or participating in parent–teacher associations can open doors to meeting other parents and exchanging parenting advice. Your neighborhood also provides an opportunity to engage with other parents., Organizing casual playdates or parent meet-ups can help you build your support network. These informal gatherings create a relaxed environment where you can talk about your concerns, celebrate milestones, and offer mutual support.

- **Utilize online platforms:** Social media groups that share parenting tips provide a space to ask questions, share your experiences, and seek counsel from a broad community. Online communities are great because they are available 24/7, so can provide support whenever you need it. Facebook groups, for instance, are a great place to connect with other parents and talk about anything from daily schedules to major concerns. There are also lots of websites and apps out there that offer expert parenting advice, forums, and interactive features. For example, sites like BabyCenter and Family Focus Blog offer useful resources. There are also apps made just for connecting with other parents in the same area, so you can set up playdates, trade off babysitting, or just have a chat over coffee. Checking out these digital resources can be a huge help if you don't have a support system in real life. It's pretty amazing how technology has made it easier for us to support each other.

- **Engage in local parenting groups:** Support groups, whether general or specific to particular parenting challenges, give you a safe space to express your frustrations, triumphs, and concerns. Attending regular meetings allows you to learn from others and gain practical advice and encouragement. For example, attending groups focused on parenting children with special needs can help you come up with specific strategies and receive emotional support unique to your circumstances. By participating in these groups, you feel less isolated, knowing others are going down similar paths. Participating in local parenting classes equips you with knowledge and opens channels for connection. For instance, Nurturing Parenting programs offer courses that emphasize building healthy relationships and effective communication. These evidence-based programs teach positive discipline strategies, helping you cultivate a nurturing environment at home. Parenting classes are often interactive, encouraging you to share your experiences and learn from each other, making them a welcoming environment for parents to connect and support each other.

- **Take advantage of local community services:** Community centers often organize fun events like movie nights, picnics, and cultural festivals that you can enjoy as a family. These events create a laid-back atmosphere where you can socialize alongside your kids and make new friends. Participating in these activities allows you to have a good time, and they are a great avenue for learning and connection.

In today's world, online resources are essential to navigate the challenges of raising children, especially when face-to-face interactions aren't always possible. From tips on handling toddler tantrums to guidance on cultivating adolescent independence, these resources cover a wide range of topics. Using online resources can enhance your parenting skills and help you stay informed on best practices.

Developing Open Lines of Communication

Effective communication is the cornerstone of healthy relationships. It nurtures connections and cultivates understanding, ensuring everyone feels heard and valued. Improving your communication skills can enhance your relationship with your children and promote a more harmonious home environment.

Let's look at some strategies to help you maintain open lines of communication.

Empathetic Listening

Empathetic listening is a key aspect of effective communication. It goes beyond just hearing the words; it's about truly understanding and connecting with the emotions behind them. When you focus on what your child is feeling rather than just half-listening, it makes a profound difference in how you interact, and you set a powerful example by showing that you care deeply about their emotions and experiences. Empathetic listening can be as simple as making eye contact, nodding, and responding with warmth and understanding, without interrupting.

When your child shares their concerns or feelings, responding with empathy—saying something like, "It sounds like you're feeling upset because..."—validates their emotions and lets them know you're truly listening. Such feedback reassures them that their emotions matter, helping them process what they're going through. As a parent, it's natural to want to jump into "fix-it" mode when your child brings up a problem, but sometimes the best thing you can do is resist the urge to offer immediate solutions. Instead, focus on making them feel heard and understood. Often, kids don't need a quick fix—they just need to know you're there, in their corner, listening and offering unwavering support.

Encouraging Expression

A crucial part of cultivating healthy communication is encouraging kids to express their emotions. One great way to do this is through emotional labeling. This simply means helping your children name their feelings. For example, if your child seems upset, you might say, "It looks like you're angry. Do you want to talk about what's going on?" This helps them recognize their emotions and teaches them how to articulate those feelings—an essential skill for effective communication.

Regularly practicing emotional labeling helps kids build a strong emotional vocabulary. The more words they have to describe what they're going through, the easier it becomes for them to share their experiences and challenges, reducing misunderstandings and conflicts along the way. Creating an environment where your kids feel safe to freely express themselves is equally important. It's all about listening with an open mind and giving them the space to experience and share their feelings.

Weekly Check-Ins

Setting up regular family discussions is a great way to improve communication and keep everyone on the same page. Family meetings offer a dedicated time for everyone to come together, talk about issues, and celebrate progress—whether it's completing daily schedules or resolving conflicts amicably. The best part? Everyone gets a say.

Making these check-ins a weekly habit shows that you prioritize open communication. During these meetings, you can brainstorm solutions, plan fun activities, or just catch up on each other's lives. This improves problem-solving skills and reinforces that every family member's voice matters.

To keep things running smoothly, have a few ground rules. Ensure everyone gets a chance to speak without being interrupted, and encourage respect for everyone's opinion. Start by sharing some good news or expressing gratitude to set a positive tone for the conversation. By making these discussions a regular thing, you'll keep communication flowing and tackle issues before they have a chance to blow up.

Open-Door Policy

Implementing an open-door policy is another effective way to promote trust and transparency within your family. An open-door policy means that your children know they can approach you anytime to discuss their concerns and challenges without fear of reprimand. This creates an environment where they feel secure and supported.

You can communicate this policy by assuring your kids that you are always available to talk about anything, no matter how difficult it may seem. Whether they want to share something exciting or need to talk about their mistakes, knowing that you will listen without immediate anger or disappointment can encourage more honest and open communication.

When your kids do come forward, you must respond calmly and constructively. For instance, if your child admits to breaking something or failing a test, instead of jumping to punishment, you can turn it into a learning opportunity and work together to find a solution. This approach shows them that you care more about their growth and well-being than about punishment.

Creating a strong support system through open communication takes time and effort, but it's worth it. By listening actively, encouraging emotional expression, scheduling regular family check-ins, and maintaining an open-door policy, you can build a deeper connection with your kids. These practices not only improve your relationships but also equip your kids with vital communication skills they'll use throughout their lives.

Building Essential Skills Through Networking

Building a strong support system and knowing when to wave the white flag and seek help are essential survival skills for effective parenting. Let's face it, sometimes you need a little backup when you're trying to decipher whether your toddler's meltdown is about world peace or because you cut their sandwich wrong.

As you move forward, remember it's crucial to identify the "I need a professional" moments—whether it's recognizing those sneaky behavioral red flags, dealing with emotional challenges, or just surviving the chaos of family relationships and parental burnout. It's okay to admit you don't have all the answers! Asking for help is a strength, not an admission of defeat, and by doing so you'll be much better equipped to manage the parenting roller coaster—and maybe even enjoy the ride.

Creating open lines of communication in your family and tapping into community resources can provide you with the care and support you need. Whether it's joining a local parenting class, scrolling through online forums (where everyone's asking the same "Is this normal?" question), or connecting with other parents at school or in your neighborhood, there's no shortage of ways to get advice and share your experience. By actively engaging with these resources and prioritizing honest, open communication, you'll build a solid support system that makes parenting an enjoyable journey.

Part IV:
Implementing Discipline With Heart

Chapter 9:

Practical Wisdom—Bringing It All Together

The greatest joy in life is seeing your children grow up to be successful adults. –
Unknown

What if parenting could feel less like a series of firefights and more like a graceful, harmonious dance—one where everyone knows the steps and feels good about them? Imagine moving through your day with your children, not constantly battling over rules and behavior but flowing together, making decisions as a team, with mutual respect and understanding. That might sound like a dream, but practical wisdom can help make it a reality. It's the secret ingredient that turns everyday parenting challenges into opportunities for growth, connection, and joy.

Applying Practical Wisdom

Practical wisdom is a mix of good decision-making, empathy, and a joyful approach to life. It allows you to parent with intention, guiding your children in a way that nurtures their independence and emotional intelligence while cultivating a calm, loving family dynamic. Rather than relying on rigid rules or reactive discipline, heart-centered discipline taps into this wisdom, focusing on teaching children how to manage their emotions and make responsible choices. It's not about perfection or control; it's about empowering kids to thrive.

One of the most powerful ways to do this is by offering children structured choices. Giving them the freedom to make decisions within certain boundaries helps them develop critical thinking skills and accountability, while also reinforcing a sense of autonomy. For example, instead of saying, "You need to do your homework now," you might ask, "Do you want to do your homework before or after dinner?" This simple shift gives your child a sense of control while still ensuring the task gets done. It teaches them to take responsibility for their choices and encourages cooperation without a battle.

Another great opportunity to use practical wisdom is during conflicts. When emotions are running high, it's easy to get frustrated and dismiss your child's feelings. But instead, try meeting their emotions with empathy and giving them a choice in how to proceed. For instance, if your child is upset because you've said no to more screen time, you could say, "I can see you're frustrated. Do you want to talk about it now, or would you rather take a few minutes to calm down and then discuss it?" This approach acknowledges their feelings, shows them that their emotions are valid, and teaches them how to handle those emotions constructively. This results in more cooperation, fewer meltdowns, and a child who feels valued. And if your child is angry because playtime has to end, instead of shutting down the conversation with a quick, "No more playing, it's bedtime," acknowledge how hard it is to stop something they enjoy and give them options—for instance, they can either help tidy up and read an extra bedtime story, or they could have a few more minutes of playtime but skip the story. Chances are, they'll calm down and consider the options you've given them. This highlights the importance of giving kids structured choices and validating their emotions, and how it can transform everyday interactions by creating a home environment where your kids feel heard and take responsibility for their actions. Over time, this will build resilience, cooperation, and emotional security, key ingredients in raising happy, confident, and well-adjusted children.

However, practical wisdom isn't just about teaching children how to behave; it's also about the energy you bring to your parenting. When you approach challenges with empathy and a sense of joy, rather than stress or frustration, you model how to handle life's ups and downs with grace. You teach your kids that mistakes are part of the learning process and that problem-solving can be a collaborative, positive experience.

Practical wisdom isn't a magic formula that makes all parenting challenges disappear, but it is a guiding philosophy that can make parenting feel more connected, purposeful, and even fun. By embracing a joyful, empathetic approach, you create an atmosphere where your kids thrive and where parenting feels more like a dance—a beautiful, collaborative movement toward growth and understanding.

Day-to-Day Scenarios and Solutions

Establishing a daily routine with structured choices gives kids a sense of control over their lives. It creates a sense of ownership and encourages them to cooperate because they know that you value their preferences.

Giving your children structured choices—for example, asking, "Would you like to wear the blue shirt or the red one today?" instead of open-ended questions like, "What do you want to wear?"—can prevent them from getting overwhelmed. This strategy nurtures confidence and autonomy within the boundaries you establish.

Below are a few techniques you can use to give your kids structured choices within boundaries, helping to build their confidence and autonomy.

Acknowledge Their Feelings

Acknowledging your children's feelings is an effective way to ease tension and build emotional intelligence. When your kids feel sad or frustrated, validating their emotions helps them feel heard and supported. For instance, saying, "I can see you're upset because we have to leave the park" shows empathy and lets them know their emotions matter. You don't have to give in to their demands, but creating a safe space for them to express themselves leads to healthier emotional regulation. Over time, when your children see that their feelings are respected, they will tend to have fewer emotional outbursts and be more cooperative.

Set Up a Quiet Corner

Setting up dedicated spaces for different activities can also improve focus and productivity. Whether it's a study area or a play zone, having a specific spot for each activity helps children know what's expected. For instance, a quiet corner with a small desk and school supplies can be used as a homework station for elementary school kids. Keeping this area free from distractions like the television or noisy siblings will enhance their ability to concentrate. Additionally, organizing the space with shelves or containers for supplies will make it easier for your kids to stay organized, which supports better academic performance and a sense of responsibility.

Create Family Rituals

Establishing a consistent winding-down ritual at the end of the day signals bedtime and prepares kids for sleep. Creating a predictable sequence of calming activities like bath time, reading a story, and dimming the lights sets the stage for relaxation. For instance, a warm bath followed by 20 minutes of reading can become a calming routine that marks the shift from active to restful time. Incorporating soothing activities like listening to soft music or practicing mindfulness exercises can enhance this sense of calm. Consistency is key; performing these rituals at the same time each night strengthens the connection between these activities and bedtime, making it easier for your children to fall asleep.

You can use these principles to create structured, practical routines that fit your family's needs:

- **For preschoolers**

    o A predictable morning routine with a wake-up time around 7:00 a.m. helps start the day smoothly. Encouraging simple tasks like brushing their teeth and washing their face sets good hygiene habits early on.

    o At breakfast, offering a choice between oatmeal with fruit or scrambled eggs can give them both a nutritional boost and a sense of control over their day.

    o Scheduling educational playtime and outdoor activities throughout the day adds structure while leaving room for flexibility.

- **For elementary school children**

    o A morning routine with added responsibilities, like packing their own school bags, helps build organizational skills.

    o After school, setting a specific hour, such as 4:00 p.m. to 5:00 p.m., for homework followed by free play balances work and leisure.

    o Dinner can be a family affair where everyone shares highlights of their day, encouraging communication and bonding.

    o Preparing for the next day by laying out clothes and packing their backpack keeps mornings hassle-free.

- **For high school students, who require more autonomy**

    o A consistent wake-up time of 7:00 a.m., paired with a solid personal care routine, sets a positive tone for the day.

    o Setting aside time for schoolwork, such as 4:00 p.m. to 6:00 p.m., helps manage their academic load.

    o Balancing extracurricular activities with relaxation is key to preventing burnout.

    o Dinner remains a valuable time for family discussions, and reviewing your kids' upcoming assignments before a 10:00 p.m. bedtime encourages responsibility while supporting their overall well-being.

Customizing the Approach to Fit Your Family

Customizing your discipline approach to match your family dynamics is key to ensuring it works and stays relevant. Here's how you can do it:

- **Align discipline strategies to your family's core values:** This will ensure the strategies are relevant and effective. When discipline methods are in harmony with a family's core values, it creates a sense of consistency that children can understand and respect. This isn't just about setting rules; it's about embodying the principles you hold dear. For instance, if you prioritize respect and empathy, your discipline strategies should reflect those values, perhaps by focusing on understanding and talking through issues rather than defaulting to punishment.

- **Set rules collaboratively:** Giving children a say in discipline cultivates a sense of ownership over their behavior. When kids have a voice in the process, they feel more accountable for their actions. This encourages cooperation and helps them understand the reasons behind certain rules. One great approach is to involve your children in setting expectations and consequences. When they help create the guidelines, they're more likely to follow them—and will also develop important communication skills along the way.

- **Consider your kids' individual needs:** Every child is different, with their own personality traits and emotional responses. Tailoring your approach to fit these differences is far more effective than using a one-size-fits-all method. For example, a sensitive child might respond better to gentle guidance, while an assertive child may need clear boundaries. Recognizing these differences allows you to apply discipline that resonates with each child's nature, making it more impactful.

Having regular discussions about what's going well and what needs improvement creates an opportunity for open dialogue. These conversations provide a chance to reflect on your experiences and make necessary adjustments. For instance, hosting a weekly family meeting can be an excellent platform to address any concerns before they escalate and to collaboratively come up with solutions. Imagine setting aside time every Sunday evening for a family meeting. During this time, everyone shares one thing that went well during the week and one area where they felt challenged. For instance, if one child expresses frustration about their homework being too overwhelming, you could all discuss ways to support that child better, such as creating dedicated homework time together or breaking assignments into smaller tasks. This proactive approach encourages teamwork and helps everyone feel heard and valued.

Finally, feedback and reflection are key to fine-tuning discipline strategies. Ask your kids for their input—questions like "How do you feel about our current rules?" or "What can we do differently?" open the door to constructive dialogue. Reflection cultivates a growth mindset and promotes continuous improvement and resilience.

Troubleshooting Common Challenges

Heart-centered discipline approaches are effective for cultivating deep emotional connections, encouraging cooperation, and promoting positive behavior in children. However, it's important to understand potential pitfalls and provide strategies to counter them. Here's how you can address possible challenges you may encounter.

Consistent Reminders Can Establish New Routines Over Time

Establishing new routines requires patience and perseverance. Consistently reminding each other of daily routines is key to embedding them into your daily life. For instance, if your child struggles with sticking to a set bedtime, gentle, regular reminders about the approaching time coupled with cues like dimming the lights or reading a bedtime story can gradually create an expectation. Using positive reinforcement rather than punitive measures encourages kids to follow rules. Over time, these consistent actions can help solidify the routine, making it part of your child's daily habits.

Visual Cues Can Serve as Reminders of Expectations and Routines

Visual cues are great tools to help kids remember what they need to do and when. For example, a chore chart on the fridge or a bright calendar with homework due dates can be helpful. These visuals are subtle but effective reminders. They work especially well for younger children who may not always understand everything said to them. By using pictures or symbols that make sense to the child, these cues become useful communication aids. For instance, a picture of a toothbrush near the bathroom can remind a child to brush their teeth before bed.

Maintaining Open Communication Builds Resilience Against Negative External Influences

Establishing open lines of communication helps kids develop resilience. Children face all kinds of external influences, from peer pressure to conflicting societal messages, which may challenge family values. Cultivating a safe space where your children feel comfortable voicing their concerns and experiences is essential. Active listening plays a key role here; validating your kids' feelings and discussing potential solutions together builds trust. For example, if your child feels pressured by peers to engage in undesirable behavior, guiding them through possible responses and practicing role-playing scenarios helps them build the confidence and skills to handle external pressures effectively.

Understanding That Relapses Are Part of Growth Can Reduce Frustration

Setbacks are a natural part of the growth process. Expecting immediate perfection in behavior changes creates unrealistic standards and can result in frustration. Instead, look at relapses as opportunities for learning rather than failures. When your child deviates from a newly established routine or guideline, approach the situation with empathy and patience. Reaffirm desired behaviors and encourage them to try again to maintain motivation. For instance, if they forget to complete their chores after successfully doing them for a week, gently reminding and supporting them can be more motivating than expressing disappointment.

Resistance to Change: Tips for Overcoming Initial Reluctance From Children

It's common for kids to push back when they're told about new rules or routines. To help them get on board, try to see things from their perspective and come up with a plan that works for everyone. Include them in the decision-making process—when kids feel like they have a voice in the changes happening in their lives, they're more likely to go along with them. For example, if you're changing their bedtime, talk to them about why it's important and see if you can find a compromise that works for both of you. Allowing them to make choices within set limits encourages them and reduces resistance.

Maintaining Consistency: Techniques for Reinforcing Consistent Practices Amid Busy Lives

Staying consistent can be difficult when life gets busy, but keeping up good habits is key to living a happier, healthier life. One way to help stay on track is by setting specific and doable goals and then sticking to them. Be clear about what you expect from your kids and lead by example. For instance, if the goal is to have family dinners together, make it a priority even when everyone's schedules are crazy. You can make it easier by prepping meals ahead of time or opting for quick, healthy options.

Addressing External Influences: Strategies for Handling Peer Pressure or Outside Opinions

Children are easily influenced by the people around them, especially their friends. It's important to teach your kids to think independently and build their self-confidence. By discussing situations where they might feel pressured by their friends and helping them come up with ways to handle such situations, you can help them feel more confident in making their own decisions. Have open conversations with your children about family values and encourage them to share their thoughts and opinions. This creates a strong and supportive environment for kids to thrive.

Dealing With Relapses: How to Bounce Back After Setbacks

It's normal to face setbacks when trying to change behavior, but the important part is knowing how to recover from setbacks for long-term success. When you experience a setback, take a moment to identify the root causes. Once you understand the reasons behind the setback, you can adjust your plan if needed and continue working toward your goal.

It's also important to stay positive and focus on the progress you've made rather than getting stuck on the setbacks. For example, if a child resorts to old behaviors, don't get discouraged. Instead, look at how far they've come and continue to support and encourage them to keep going. Remember, setbacks are a natural part of the change process and, with perseverance and a positive mindset, you can overcome them and reach your goals.

Implementing Heart-Centered Discipline Strategies

As we wrap up this chapter, take a moment to reflect on the strategies we've discussed and how you can incorporate them into your family routine. How can you start nurturing will, wisdom, and joy in your family?

Remember, the beauty of these principles lies in their adaptability. Tailoring them to fit your family's unique dynamics means you can create routines that resonate with everyone. Structuring your mornings, incorporating educational playtime, and keeping lines of communication open will promote cooperation and resilience. If you're navigating the complexities of raising adolescents, finding that sweet balance between academic responsibilities and relaxation is crucial. This balance can alleviate stress and promote well-being.

As you continue this journey, keep in mind that adjusting your approach to discipline to match your children's temperaments is essential for their relevance and effectiveness. Regular check-ins and open discussions create a warm, supportive environment where your kids feel understood and appreciated. This foundation will empower your family to handle changes together, with empathy and compassion at the forefront.

Remember, every small step you take creates ripples of positivity, shaping not just your children's lives but your entire family dynamic.

Chapter 10:
Growing Together—Evolving as a Family

I don't think anyone can grow unless he's loved exactly as he is now, appreciated for what he is rather than what he will be. –Fred Rogers

Every family is a dynamic, ever-changing unit. As children grow and parents evolve, the needs, challenges, and joys naturally shift, requiring everyone to adapt. But at the heart of these transitions lies an incredible opportunity to grow together, learn from one another, and reinforce the bonds that keep the family close. As we go through this ever-evolving process, we find that growth isn't just an individual journey; it's a collective experience that brings the family closer and strengthens parent–child relationships.

Take the example of the Martins, a family with two young children aged five and eight. As their kids entered different developmental stages, the Martins realized that the approach they had used when their children were toddlers no longer worked. Time-outs and simple "nos" were met with defiance and frustration as their children began to assert their independence. It felt like the relationship was changing overnight, and the parents found themselves constantly on edge, unsure of how to restore balance.

One evening, after a particularly rough day filled with sibling bickering and endless negotiations over screen time, Mrs. Martin sat down with her husband to rethink their approach. They decided to try a different strategy. Instead of focusing on punishing their kids and setting rules, they devised a plan to have more open conversations with their children. The following week, they gathered the kids after dinner and explained that the family was going to work together to find new ways of solving problems and respecting each other's feelings. They even encouraged their children to share their thoughts and ideas on how they could work as a team.

At first, the kids were skeptical, but over time, something remarkable happened: The children started to voice their concerns more calmly and even came up with solutions when conflicts arose. Power struggles became a thing of the past as the family learned to collaborate. The Martins discovered that adjusting their approach and communicating openly not only resolved conflicts more effectively but also created an environment where everyone felt appreciated.

In this chapter, we will explore the beautiful process of evolving as a family, where growth becomes a shared experience. Heart-centered discipline, like the approach the Martins adopted, is just one part of the equation. Open communication, mutual support, and a genuine commitment to understanding one another are essential in managing life's inevitable changes.

Every family member, whether it's you trying to balance boundaries and connection or your kids learning to express their feelings, has the chance to grow together. Through this collective growth, your family bond will deepen and you will create a dynamic that thrives on trust and love, while life's challenges and transitions will become opportunities for deeper understanding and stronger relationships. By embracing these shifts with open hearts and minds, you can evolve into a more connected, empathetic, and joyful family.

By implementing these strategies, you'll build a relationship that not only survives the inevitable changes of life but thrives on them, growing stronger through each challenge, joy, and milestone.

Navigating Changes and Challenges

Navigating the journey of family life is all about growing together—parents and kids alike. As your children move through different stages, things will naturally shift at home, and everyone has to adapt. That's not just a challenge; it's an opportunity to strengthen your bond and build resilience. Think of big changes like moving to a new home or your child starting school. Instead of seeing them as disruptions, you can turn these moments into powerful learning experiences that bring your family closer.

As you go through different transitions:

- **View them as opportunities for growth:** Transitions can be transformative. They can help you build resilience and adaptability within your family. For example, when your child starts school, it can be exciting and challenging. Instead of focusing solely on the logistical changes, you can embrace the moment by discussing the new environment, meeting teachers together, and creating routines that support your child's success. This approach eases their adjustment and strengthens the family as you work together to face new challenges.

- **Address challenges proactively:** Strategies like conflict resolution plans can help mitigate common family issues. Open discussions about matters that affect you allow everyone to voice concerns and work together to find solutions. These sessions encourage open communication and teach kids valuable negotiation and empathy skills, creating a more cooperative and supportive home environment.

- **Cultivate resilience:** Building resilience together involves celebrating small victories and teaching coping skills. Recognizing everyday achievements, like completing chores or doing well on a test, enhances morale and reinforces positive behavior. Acknowledging the effort kids put into completing tasks promotes a sense of accomplishment and motivates them to continue striving for their best. Additionally, teaching coping skills like mindfulness, deep breathing, or keeping a gratitude journal equips them with tools to manage stress effectively.

- **Proactively manage transitions and challenges:** Teaching children to view changes as opportunities for growth prepares them for future experiences. This is especially important during significant life stages, like adolescence, when the need for autonomy and guidance becomes critical. Proactively addressing these needs ensures that your family remains a strong support system, ready to grow and adapt together.

Discussing emotions also helps your kids develop emotional intelligence. They will learn to express their feelings and understand other people, which is crucial for social development. You can also gain insights into your children's inner world, enhancing your parenting strategies. These conversations prevent the buildup of unresolved emotions that could lead to larger conflicts, cultivating a family atmosphere built on openness, trust, and emotional security.

Resilience is built not only by facing challenges together but also by recognizing the strength you gain from overcoming those challenges. Whether it's a health issue or a financial setback, facing crises as a family shows the importance of unity and collective strength. These experiences remind you that you can weather future storms together.

Teaching coping skills is another key to building resilience. You can integrate practical techniques like problem-solving, emotional regulation, and stress management into your daily family life. Practicing calm-down techniques during moments of frustration, for example, helps you and your kids manage your emotions more effectively. By sharing and practicing these skills regularly, your children will learn to handle stress independently while remaining a part of a supportive network.

Continuing the Journey of Heart-Centered Discipline

Heart-centered discipline is an evolving practice that adapts to the changing dynamics of family life. While the core principles remain the same, the way you apply them must shift in response to your kids' developmental stages and emerging research. Staying flexible ensures that your discipline approach remains relevant and effective over time, creating a nurturing environment where your family relationships can flourish.

Here are a few strategies you can implement as you continue this journey:

- **View discipline as a continuous learning process:** As your family grows, whether that's welcoming new members or adapting to different life stages, change will bring unique challenges and opportunities. Discipline, therefore, should be seen not as a static set of rules but as a flexible approach that adapts as your family evolves. For example, strategies that worked well when your child was a toddler will need to be adjusted as they grow older. Recognizing this helps you remain responsive and attuned to your children's ever-changing needs.

- **Stay informed about new research in child development:** By staying up-to-date with advancements in our understanding of emotional regulation, cognitive development, and effective discipline strategies, you can refine your approaches based on proven methods. For instance, recent studies highlight the importance of positive reinforcement and the harmful effects of punitive measures on a child's emotional well-being (Morin, 2024). By integrating these findings, you can create a more nurturing and supportive atmosphere for your kids.

- **Share discipline experiences with your family and other parents:** Open communication about effective and ineffective discipline approaches creates an environment where you can share insights and learn from the experiences of other parents. Whether through parenting groups or casual conversations with friends and family, these discussions provide valuable support. For instance, if you've found a successful way to manage tantrums, sharing it with fellow parents facing similar challenges can be incredibly helpful. By exchanging experiences, you gain fresh perspectives and practical solutions that can be adapted to different situations, enhancing your approach to parenting.

Anticipating future developmental stages with a heart-centered approach involves preparing for upcoming transitions. As children grow, their needs and behaviors change. Planning for these changes helps you respond proactively rather than reactively. For example, as your child approaches adolescence, you can focus on cultivating open communication, encouraging independence, and maintaining a supportive presence. This forward-thinking approach ensures a stable environment that adapts to their evolving needs.

Implementing Heartfelt Discipline Principles Effectively

- **Re-evaluate your discipline strategies:** Regularly assess and adjust your discipline strategies based on your children's current needs and behaviors. What worked in the past may not be suitable as your kids grow. Stay attuned to their developmental changes and be willing to adapt your approach accordingly. Reflecting on and revising your strategies ensures they remain effective over time.

- **Integrate new learning:** Commit to ongoing education about child development and effective parenting practices. Attend workshops, read books, and engage with reputable sources to stay informed about the latest research. Incorporate these new insights into your daily interactions with your children. For instance, if new studies highlight the benefits of cultivating emotional intelligence, ask yourself, "How can I integrate activities and conversations that promote emotional awareness and regulation into our daily lives?"

- **Share experiences:** Cultivate a culture of open communication within your family. Encourage your kids to share their experiences with discipline, including both positive and negative, and create a safe space where they are comfortable sharing their thoughts and feelings. This allows you to learn from each other and understand which strategies are effective. This teamwork effort can deepen your family bond and promote a sense of unity.

- **Prepare for future challenges:** Anticipate the developmental stages your children will go through and prepare for the challenges you may encounter. Research typical behaviors and needs for each stage and devise strategies to address them in advance. This forward-thinking approach will enable you to create methods to guide your children through different transitions smoothly. For example, if you know your child will soon start school, discuss the changes and expectations early on, helping them feel prepared and confident.

Approaching discipline as a continuous journey of learning and adaptation will help you create an environment where everyone feels supported and appreciated. Preparing for future challenges with a heart-centered mindset cultivates emotional wellness, cooperation, and respect, laying the foundation for a thriving family life.

Adapting to Each Developmental Stage

Adapting your parenting strategies to match your children's developmental stages is key to maintaining a nurturing environment. This ensures that you support them based on their growth and evolving needs, promoting emotional and psychological well-being.

Here are a few strategies to help you adapt your parenting approach effectively:

- **Understand key developmental milestones:** This is the first step in setting realistic expectations and giving your kids the support they need. Learning about these milestones allows you to anticipate changes and plan your responses. For example, toddlers start trying out their independence by walking and talking, which requires a secure yet exploration-friendly environment. As children reach school age, they develop cognitive and social skills like reading and making friends. Recognizing these milestones helps you create an environment conducive to learning and emotional security.

- **Develop age-appropriate discipline strategies:** Young children respond well to clear, immediate consequences like time-outs or the withdrawal of privileges for misbehavior. In contrast, adolescents benefit from more nuanced approaches, such as discussing responsibilities and consequences. Adapt your discipline strategies as your kids evolve. For example, while younger children might need straightforward rules, older children are more likely to respond positively when they are involved in setting rules, which cultivates a sense of ownership and accountability.

- **Balance independence with guidance:** As your kids demonstrate readiness, gradually give them more responsibilities so they can start to develop independence while still relying on your support. For younger kids, this could involve simple tasks like dressing themselves or choosing snacks, while adolescents might take on larger roles such as managing their schedules or assisting with household chores. Allowing your children to solve problems on their own, stepping in only when necessary, helps them develop problem-solving skills and nurtures independence.

- **Maintain open communication:** As children grow, the parent–child relationship evolves, and talking about these shifts is necessary. Early childhood often requires you to take on a more directive role, setting boundaries and guiding behavior. As your children enter adolescence, your relationship shifts toward a partnership based on mutual respect and understanding. Talking about these changes can ease confusion and frustration. For example, explaining why a previous bedtime routine no longer applies to a teenager helps them understand and accept the evolving relationship.

- **Be flexible:** It's also important to remain flexible, recognizing that each child is unique and may develop at their own pace.

Tailoring your parenting strategies to individual temperaments allows you to personalize your approach. By adapting your parenting techniques to suit each child's personality, you can better support their development.

- **Understand the link between emotional needs and behavior:** Children often express their needs through behavior, reflecting whether your current parenting approaches are effective. For instance, if your child constantly complains about restrictive rules, this could indicate that they feel over-controlled and are ready for more autonomy. Conversely, if your child constantly asks for help, it could be that they need more support and guidance.

- **Set guidelines specific to each developmental stage:** For toddlers, establishing consistent routines and clear boundaries is essential. Simple instructions and immediate feedback make it easier for kids to understand your expectations. Allowing school-aged children to make choices within set limits helps them develop decision-making skills and builds confidence. Adolescents, on the other hand, thrive when you adopt a collaborative approach. Allowing them to contribute to setting rules and expectations encourages maturity and mutual respect.

Creating shared experiences is a great way to support your children's growing autonomy while maintaining a strong connection. Family activities like game nights, outings, or collaborative projects provide opportunities to bond and allow you to have conversations about the changes that come with growth. These moments deepen your connections while also cultivating respect for each other's independence.

Finally, addressing changes in your family requires acknowledging that family life is ever-evolving. Remain adaptable, knowing that what works at one stage may need to be adjusted as your children grow. Celebrating milestones, acknowledging your achievements, and supporting one another through transitions are key to building a strong relationship.

Embracing Change

Family life is an ever-changing journey of learning, growth, and connection. Embracing the dynamic nature of family relationships allows you to easily adapt to your children's changing needs. Rather than seeing transitions and challenges as obstacles, view them as chances to grow together, building resilience and encouraging cooperation along the way. By prioritizing open communication and working together to solve problems, you create an environment where everyone feels heard and valued. This ongoing dialogue nurtures emotional well-being and strengthens your family bond.

Adjusting your parenting strategies to meet your children where they are in their development is crucial to maintaining harmony. Anticipating and understanding these stages helps you create strategies that support growth while encouraging independence. Celebrating small wins and practicing coping skills together cultivates a sense of resilience, creating a space where your kids feel empowered to face life's challenges with confidence.

By staying flexible and responsive, you can handle the twists and turns of growth with empathy and understanding, ensuring a loving and stable environment for your kids.

Conclusion

My understanding of the way a child grows is that you create the garden, you don't grow the flower. You can merely fertilize the earth and keep it soft and moist, and then the flower grows as best it can. –Ram Dass

As we conclude this book, remember that this is just the beginning of a transformative journey—one that invites you to nurture, guide, and grow alongside your children with compassion and wisdom. The principles you've explored here are not quick fixes but lasting foundations for a family built on love, trust, and mutual respect. Each day offers a new opportunity to practice heart-centered discipline, and with every step, you are shaping the kind of future your children will carry forward.

So, as you close this book, know that the real story is just beginning—the story of a family rooted in connection, where discipline leads not only to better behavior but also to meaningful relationships. The heart of parenting beats stronger with each mindful choice you make. Through these pages, we've explored heart-centered discipline—a philosophy that places emotional well-being and meaningful connection at the forefront of parenting. You've gathered tools and insights that can transform your parenting approach and your family.

Think back to the challenging moments you've experienced with your child—times when your patience was tested or when you struggled to respond with compassion. These moments are not signs of failure but growth opportunities. They invite you to ask yourself, "Am I creating an environment that encourages growth for me and my kids?" Embrace every experience—not just the easy ones, but the difficult ones too—as a chance to deepen your connection and understanding. Heart-centered discipline isn't about perfection; it's about progress and presence.

Now, take a moment to envision the future. Picture a home where laughter fills the rooms, misunderstandings are met with patience, and everyone feels heard, valued, and respected. This vision is not out of reach—it's the future you're creating through heart-centered discipline. By prioritizing empathy, respect, and cooperation today, you're building the foundation for loving and supportive relationships that will last a lifetime. Imagine the ripple effect this can have, not only within your family but for generations to come. The seeds of connection you plant now will grow into something beautiful and long-lasting.

Parenting is an ever-evolving journey, and your role will change as your kids grow. Over time, you'll need to adapt some of the strategies you've learned here. In the early years of your kids' development, you might rely on gentle guidance; as your kids grow, you'll shift to setting firm yet empathetic boundaries. By staying attuned to your children's changing needs and educating yourself, you'll ensure that your parenting approach remains effective.

Remember, you are not just a teacher but a learner on this journey, evolving alongside your child. One of the most impactful ways to sustain this approach is by building a support network. Parenting often feels isolating, especially when you're facing unique challenges. But imagine being part of a community where parents come together to share their experiences, insights, and encouragement. Whether it's through local groups, online forums, or casual gatherings, these connections remind you that you're not alone. Together, you can support each other, growing stronger and more resilient in your shared journey.

At its core, heart-centered discipline is about recognizing the humanity in yourself and your kids. It's about understanding that mistakes are a natural part of learning, and that compassion can guide you through the toughest times.

The journey doesn't end here; it continues with every interaction, every choice, and every moment of reflection. Embrace each challenge as a chance to practice what you've learned and to build a deeper, more meaningful relationship with your kids. As you move forward, keep in mind that the essence of heart-centered discipline lies in consistent empathy, patience, and respect. It's about creating a home where your children feel safe to express themselves and know they will be met with understanding instead of judgment. This approach improves behavior and nurtures emotional intelligence, resilience, and a strong sense of belonging in kids.

Take a moment to visualize the day when your grown child looks back on their childhood with gratitude for the love, understanding, and support that shaped them. Picture the pride you'll feel knowing you've equipped them with the emotional and social skills they need to handle life's challenges. By committing to heart-centered discipline now, you are planting seeds that will grow into lifelong relationships built on trust and mutual respect.

This journey requires dedication and personal transformation. You may need to unlearn old patterns and replace them with more constructive habits. Change doesn't happen overnight, but with persistence and a commitment to growth, you'll begin to see positive shifts. Celebrate the small victories along the way, and approach setbacks with grace rather than self-criticism. Your desire to become a better parent is, in itself, an expression of deep love.

In closing, heart-centered discipline is a path of continuous learning, reflection, and connection. It calls for compassion not only toward your children but also toward yourself. Embrace this philosophy with an open heart, reflect on your growth, and stay committed to learning and building social connections. By doing so, you will shape your family's future and contribute to a more compassionate and connected world.

References

Abimbola, E. (2024, March 26). *Fostering positive discipline through empathy*. IBelieve. https://www.ibelieve.com/motherhood/fostering-positive-discipline-through-empathy.html

Aguilar, E. (2011, September 23). *20 tips for developing positive relationships with parents*. Edutopia. https://www.edutopia.org/blog/20-tips-developing-positive-relationships-parents-elena-aguilar

Ávila, S. C. (2022, March 30). *Understanding forgiveness in children and adolescents*. Templeton World Charity Foundation. https://www.templetonworldcharity.org/blog/understanding-forgiveness-children-and-adolescents

Bach, R. (n.d.). Quote. In Jones, W. (2024, May 17). *57 family inspirational quotes for strength and unity*. PsychicBlaze. https://psychicblaze.com/family-inspirational-quotes/

Bai, S., & Repetti, R. L. (2015). Short-term resilience processes in the family. *Family Relations*, *64*(1), 108–119. https://doi.org/10.1111/fare.12101

Bean, S. (n.d.). *How to improve your child's behavior and regain control as a parent*. Empowering Parents. https://www.empoweringparents.com/article/in-over-your-head-how-to-improve-your-childs-behavior-and-regain-control-as-a-parent/

Bell, J., & Condren, M. (2016). Communication strategies for empowering and protecting children. *The Journal of Pediatric Pharmacology and Therapeutics*, *21*(2), 176–184. https://doi.org/10.5863/1551-6776-21.2.176

Boryga, A. (2022, August 5). *For young kids, the power of play-based learning.* Edutopia. https://www.edutopia.org/article/young-kids-power-play-based-learning/

Brown, B. (n.d.). *Brené Brown quote.* In Tingley, L. (2021, June 6). *100 positive parenting quotes about raising children.* Simply Well Balanced. https://simply-well-balanced.com/positive-parenting-quotes/

Campbell, A. (2024, July 3). *Fostering emotional development in our children: How emotional intelligence can change the way we parent.* Momwell. https://www.momwell.com/blog/fostering-emotional-development-in-our-children

Center on the Developing Child, Harvard University. (n.d.). *InBrief: The science of early childhood development.* (n.d.). https://developingchild.harvard.edu/resources/inbrief-science-of-ecd/

Cloud, H. (n.d.). *Henry Cloud quotes.* Goodreads. https://www.goodreads.com/work/quotes/1393909-boundaries-with-kids

Colorado Christian University. (n.d.). *Building strong parent–teacher relationships.* https://www.ccu.edu/blogs/cags/category/education/building-strong-parent-teacher-relationships/

Croteau, J. (2024, July 29). *What is restorative justice in schools? Everything educators need to know.* We Are Teachers. https://www.weareteachers.com/restorative-justice/

Dass, R. (n.d.). Quote. In Lagacé, M. (n.d.). *100 parenting quotes to encourage and inspire you.* Wisdom Quotes. https://wisdomquotes.com/parenting-quotes/

Eanes, R. (n.d.). *The importance of boundaries with kids and how to set them.* Creative Child.

https://www.creativechild.com/articles/view/the-importance-of-boundaries-with-kids-and-how-to-set-them

Elbeltagi, R., Al-Beltagi, M., Saeed, N. K., & Alhawamdeh, R. (2023). Play therapy in children with autism: Its role, implications, and limitations. *World Journal of Clinical Pediatrics*, *12*(1), 1–22. https://www.ncbi.nlm.nih.gov/pmc/articles/PMC9850869/

Engel, B. (2002, July 1). *The power of apology*. Psychology Today. https://www.psychologytoday.com/us/articles/200207/the-power-apology

Ford, T. (n.d.). Quote. In Smith, T. (2022, November 4). *55 connection quotes that bind us together*. Happier Human. https://www.happierhuman.com/connection-quotes/

Frosch, C. A., Schoppe-Sullivan, S. J., & O'Banion, D. D. (2019). Parenting and child development: A relational health perspective. *American Journal of Lifestyle Medicine*, *15*(1), 45–59. https://doi.org/10.1177/1559827619849028

Ginsburg, K. R., Committee on Communications, & Committee on Psychosocial Aspects of Child and Family Health. (2007). The importance of play in promoting healthy child development and maintaining strong parent-child bonds. *Pediatrics*, *119*(1), 182–191. https://doi.org/10.1542/peds.2006-2697

Gowmon, V. (n.d.). *Inspiring quotes on child learning and development*. Vince Gowmon. https://www.vincegowmon.com/inspiring-quotes-on-child-learning-and-development/

Grebelsky-Lichtman, T., & Shenker, E. (2017). Patterns of nonverbal parental communication: A social and situational contexts approach. *Journal of Social and Personal Relationships*, *36*(1), 83–108. https://doi.org/10.1177/0265407517719502

Guy-Evans, O. (2024, January 28). *Dopamine function in the brain.* Simply Psychology. https://www.simplypsychology.org/the-role-of-dopamine-as-a-neurotransmitter-in-the-human-brain.html

Hewitt, A. (2023, October 7). *The delicate balancing act of parenting.* Medium. https://medium.com/modern-women/the-delicate-balancing-act-of-parenting-63369695abcf

Housman Institute. (2019, November 15). *Science-backed benefits of practicing gratitude with kids.* https://www.housmaninstitute.com/blog/science-backed-benefits-of-practicing-gratitude-with-kids

How family counseling can teach you effective discipline strategies. (2024, May 24). M Kim O'Connor & Associates. https://mkimoconnor.com/how-family-counseling-in-westchester-county-new-york-can-teach-you-effective-discipline-strategies/

Importance of parents modeling emotional intelligence. (n.d.). Solobo. https://solobotoys.com/blogs/solobo/parental-modeling-of-emotional-intelligence

The importance of positive reinforcement: Celebrating your child's achievements. (n.d.). EverydayEducate. https://everydayeducate.com/blogs/news/the-importance-of-positive-reinforcement-celebrating-your-childs-achievements

Inspired New Horizons. (2022, February 5). *The transformational power of an apology.* https://inspirednewhorizons.com/2022/02/05/the-transformational-power-of-an-apology/

Karni-Visel, Y., Hershkowitz, I., Lamb, M. E., & Blasbalg, U. (2021). Nonverbal emotions while disclosing child abuse: The role of interviewer support. *Child Maltreatment, 28*(1), 66–75. https://doi.org/10.1177/10775595211063497

Kim, A., Sutthipong, P., LeVaughn, M., & Osier, N. D. (2023). Brain chemicals that make us happy or sad. *Frontiers for Young Minds*, *11*, 1023491. https://doi.org/10.3389/frym.2023.1023491

King, M. L., Jr. (n.d.). Quote. In Medrut, F. (2022, September 14). *51 forgiveness quotes to help you let go and move on*. Goalcast. https://www.goalcast.com/forgiveness-quotes/

Lasecke, M., Baeza-Hernandez, K., Dosovitsky, G., DeBellis, A., Bettencourt, B., Park, A. L., & Bunge, E. L. (2022). Disseminating online parenting resources in the community during the COVID-19 pandemic: Lessons learned. *Journal of Community Psychology*, *50*(5), 2443–2457. https://doi.org/10.1002/jcop.22788

Lerner, C. (2021, February 1). *Understanding and supporting highly sensitive children (HSC)*. Lerner Child Development. https://www.lernerchilddevelopment.com/mainblog/2018/7/25/ddnt-ever-say-that-to-me-again-do-you-understand-do-you-understand-how-to-respond-to-highly-sensitive-reactive-children

Leyba, E. (2019, December 27). *10 daily rituals that help parents bond with young children*. Psychology Today. https://www.psychologytoday.com/us/blog/joyful-parenting/201912/10-daily-rituals-help-parents-bond-young-children

Lisa. (2024, April 26). *Empathetic parenting: Raising emotionally intelligent children*. ABF Creative. https://www.abfc.co/empathetic-parenting-raising-emotionally-intelligent-children/

MacPhee, D., Lunkenheimer, E., & Riggs, N. (2015). Resilience as regulation of developmental and family processes. *Family Relations*, *64*(1), 153–175. https://doi.org/10.1111/fare.12100

Malik, F., & Marwaha, R. (n.d.). *Developmental stages of social-emotional development in children.* StatPearls Publishing. https://www.ncbi.nlm.nih.gov/books/NBK534819/

McCullough, M. E. (2001). Forgiveness: Who does it and how do they do it? *Current Directions in Psychological Science, 10*(6), 194–197. https://doi.org/10.1111/1467-8721.00147

McKee, L. G., Algoe, S. B., Faro, A. L., O'Leary, J. L., & O'Neal, C. W. (2019). Picture this! Bringing joy into focus and developing healthy habits of mind: Rationale, design, and implementation of a randomized control trial for young adults. *Contemporary Clinical Trials Communications, 15,* 100391. https://doi.org/10.1016/j.conctc.2019.100391

Melbourne Child Psychology & School Psychology Services. (n.d.). *Adapting your parenting style for your child's developmental stage.* (n.d.). https://melbournechildpsychology.com.au/blog/adapting-your-parenting-style-for-your-childs-developmental-stage/

Miller, B. (n.d.). Quote. In Vallejo, M. (2024, September 9). *50 parenting quotes to inspire and guide.* Mental Health Center Kids. https://mentalhealthcenterkids.com/blogs/articles/parenting-quotes

Morin, A. (2024, April 16). *How positive reinforcement encourages good behavior in kids.* Parents. https://www.parents.com/positive-reinforcement-examples-8619283

Morris, A. S., Hays-Grudo, J., Kerr, K. L., & Beasley, L. O. (2021). The heart of the matter: Developing the whole child through community resources and caregiver relationships. *Development and Psychopathology, 33*(2), 533–544. https://doi.org/10.1017/s0954579420001595

National Academies of Sciences, Engineering, and Medicine; Division of Behavioral and Social Sciences and Education; Board on

Children, Youth, and Families; Committee on Supporting the Parents of Young Children; Breiner H, Ford M, Gadsden VL (Eds.). (2016). *Parenting matters: Supporting parents of children ages 0–8*. National Academies Press (US). https://www.ncbi.nlm.nih.gov/books/NBK402020

National Research Council (US), Institute of Medicine (US) Committee on Integrating the Science of Early Childhood Development, Shonkoff, J. P., & Phillips, D. A. (2000). *From neurons to neighborhoods: The science of early childhood development*. National Academies Press (US). https://www.ncbi.nlm.nih.gov/books/NBK225562/

Nelsen, J. (n.d.). *The importance of connection*. Positive Discipline. https://www.positivediscipline.com/articles/importance-connection

Nivison, M., Deneault, A.-A., & Madigan, S. (2023, October 19). *How children's secure attachment sets the stage for positive well-being*. The Conversation. https://theconversation.com/how-childrens-secure-attachment-sets-the-stage-for-positive-well-being-213423

Nurturing Parenting. (2023, October 26). *The ultimate guide to effective parenting programs*. https://www.nurturingparenting.com/blog/the-ultimate-guide-to-effective-parenting-programs/

Parental burnout: Causes, signs, & how to cope. (2024, January 30). Sedona Sky Academy. https://www.sedonasky.org/blog/parental-burnout

Parenting with the HEART in mind. (n.d.). HEART in Mind. https://loreamartinez.com/parenting/

Playful parenting tips. (n.d.). Marbles Kids Museum. https://www.marbleskidsmuseum.org/playful-parenting-tips

Positive Action Team. (2024, October 8). *Empowering students with effective decision-making skills: A how-to guide.* Positive Action. https://www.positiveaction.net/blog/empowering-students-with-effective-decision-making-skills

Positive discipline and guidance for children. (n.d) AbilityPath. https://abilitypath.org/ap-resources/positive-discipline-and-guidance-for-children/

Raj, P., Elizabeth, C. S., & Padmakumari, P. (2016). Mental health through forgiveness: Exploring the roots and benefits. *Cogent Psychology, 3*(1). https://doi.org/10.1080/23311908.2016.1153817

Reed, C. (2023, July 3). *Responsible independence: Giving your child their freedom - saddleback parents.* Saddleback Parents. https://onpurposeparents.com/responsible-independence-giving-your-child-their-freedom/

Restorative practices in schools: Designing for equity. (n.d.). Next Generation Learning Challenges. https://www.nextgenlearning.org/equity-toolkit/school-culture

Richard. (2023, April 20). *The value of teaching your child to be financially responsible.* Sprott Learning. https://sprottlearning.com/kids/the-value-of-teaching-your-child-to-be-financially-responsible

Rodgers, L. (n.d.). *When and how babies lift their heads up*. What to Expect. https://www.whattoexpect.com/first-year/lift-head/

Rogers, F. (n.d.). Quote. In Lagacé, M. *100 parenting quotes to encourage and inspire you.* Wisdom Quotes. https://wisdomquotes.com/parenting-quotes/

Samora, J. (2023, September 17). *10 family therapy activities for building relationships.* Healing Collective Therapy.

https://healingcollectivetherapy.com/resources/family-therapy-activities

Sautter, E. (n.d.). *How gratitude builds emotional intelligence in neurodivergent kids & teens.* Elizabeth Sautter. https://elizabethsautter.com/how-gratitude-builds-emotional-intelligence-in-neurodiverse-children-and-teens/

Setting boundaries with kids and how it's done. (2024, January 12). Conscious Mommy. https://www.consciousmommy.com/post/setting-boundaries-with-children-how-to

Shabbir, R. (n.d.). *20 math games that make math learning fun.* Educationise. https://educationise.com/post/20-math-games-that-make-math-learning-fun/

Souders, B. (2024, July 26). *Positive reinforcement for kids: 11+ examples for parents.* PositivePsychology.com. https://positivepsychology.com/parenting-positive-reinforcement/

Stanford Medical Children's Health. (n.d.). *Cognitive development in the teen years.* https://www.stanfordchildrens.org/en/topic/default?id=cognitive-development-in-adolescence-90-P01594

Sutton, J. (2024, July 17). *Family conflict resolution: 6 worksheets & scenarios (+ PDF).* PositivePsychology.com. https://positivepsychology.com/conflict-resolution-family-kids/

Swindoll, C. R. (n.d.). *Charles R. Swindoll quote.* BrainyQuote. https://www.brainyquote.com/quotes/charles_r_swindoll_106981

Tauscher, S. (n.d.). Quote. In Gowman, V. (n.d.). *Inspiring quotes on child learning and development.* Vince Gowmon.

https://www.vincegowmon.com/inspiring-quotes-on-child-learning-and-development/

Teenagers and communication. (2012). Better Health Channel. https://www.betterhealth.vic.gov.au/health/healthyliving/teenagers-and-communication

Todorov, G. (2023, June 2). *25 best parenting blogs and websites [to Follow] in 2024.* ThriveMyWay. https://thrivemyway.com/parenting-blogs/

Top 10 ways parents can help their kids prepare for the new school year. (n.d.). Peachey Counselling and Family Support. https://www.peacheycounselling.ca/blog/2024/top-10-ways-parents-can-help-their-kids-get-ready-for-the-new-school-year

12 essential conflict resolution skills for kids: Tools for peaceful problem-solving. (n.d.). WholeHearted School Counseling. https://wholeheartedschoolcounseling.com/2023/05/05/12-conflict-resolution-skills-for-kids-helping-children-become-independent-problem-solvers/

Unknown. (n.d.). Quote. In Flatley, K. (n.d.). *70 of the most popular quotes for parents that sum up what parenting is really like.* Self-Sufficient Kids. https://selfsufficientkids.com/quotes-for-parents/

van der Wal, R. C., Levelt, L., Kluwer, E., & Finkenauer, C. (2024). Exploring associations between children's forgiveness following parental divorce and psychological well-being. *Family Transitions*, 65(3), 248–270. https://doi.org/10.1080/28375300.2024.2310432

Via. (2009, April 9). *10 basic principles of good parenting: Notes & review.* Vialogue. https://vialogue.wordpress.com/2009/04/09/10-basic-principles-of-good-parenting-notes-review/

What is parental burnout and what can you do about it? (n.d.). The Relationship Place. https://www.sdrelationshipplace.com/signs-of-parental-burnout/

Williamson. (2023, August 21). *Unlocking the power of play-based learning: 20 engaging activities for holistic development.* School Life Diaries. https://web.archive.org/web/20240305012731/https://schoollifediaries.com/play-based-learning/

www.ingramcontent.com/pod-product-compliance
Lightning Source LLC
Chambersburg PA
CBHW040233110526
44582CB00002B/44